SPANISH-ENGLISH
ENGLISH-SPANISH
(LATIN AMERICAN)
DICTIONARY AND PHRASEBOOK

SPANISH-ENGLISH
ENGLISH-SPANISH
(LATIN AMERICAN)
DICTIONARY AND PHRASEBOOK

ILA WARNER

HIPPOCRENE BOOKS
New York

ISBN 0-7818-0773-5

For information, address:
HIPPOCRENE BOOKS, INC.
171 Madison Avenue
New York, NY 10016

Printed in the United States of America.

Many thanks to Juanita Flores for her invaluable help in taming "the monster," i.e. the author's unfathomable computer.

CONTENTS

INTRODUCTION

The purpose of this dictionary and phrasebook is to provide the English-speaking traveler to Latin America with a concise and practical tool for basic communication in Spanish.

The words in the dictionary section were carefully selected to include:The most basic function words such as articles, prepositions and personal pronouns; the nouns and verbs most necessary for the casual traveler; and vocabulary useful to the business traveler.

This section only lists the most common meanings of words, those most essential for moving around Latin America. For example, it is useful to know that the word *caballeros* means "gentlemen" as this is how the men's room is often labeled. It is of no use at all, however, for the traveler to know that the word also means "knights."

All vocabulary is presented with its phonetic pronunciation. In addition, a brief outline of the rules of Spanish pronunciation is provided. Those who have, at some point, studied Spanish may find that a review of this section is all they need.

This guide also includes a very abbreviated overview of the most basic elements of Spanish grammar. Of necessity, many complicated structures have been omitted, even when touched upon in the dictionary section. For example, a number of verbs that appear in the dictionary section are reflexive, that is, they reflect the action back to the subject. They can be identified by the little word *se* attached to the infinitive form. Of necessity, this detail must be included as it often impacts the meaning of the verb. For example, the verb *llamar* means "to call," while its reflexive form *llamarse* means "to be called, or named." However, no explanation of reflexives is included in the grammar section. They are just too complex to fall within the scope of this book.

Differences in usage from one Latin American country to another appear in both the dictionary and phrasebook sections of this guide. Diplomats and housewives, professionals and factory workers from the various regions of Latin America provided all the information on usage that is included in this book. Only the people who live in Latin America and speak the Spanish of their respective regions are truly reliable sources of this type of information. The differences included here, of course, are in no way exhaustive.

The goal of this book is to present essential language information in the simplest and most useful format possible. It is our hope that this has been accomplished.

A BRIEF HISTORY OF THE SPANISH LANGUAGE

Its Origins in the Old World

The Spanish language, spoken in nineteen countries of Latin America, had its origins on the Iberian peninsula, today the site of Spain and Portugal. Its origins date from the third century B.C. with the arrival of the Romans on that peninsula. With them, they brought the language known as vulgar Latin, that is, the Latin spoken by the common people of the day in contrast to classical Latin. The Spanish spoken today by some one hundred million people evolved from that language.

In the 5TH century A.D., Germanic tribes from the north of Europe invaded all of the Roman Empire including the Iberian peninsula. But as these tribes, the Visigoths, were very primitive they came to adopt the more advanced language and culture of the conquered rather than imposing their own.

The arrival of the Moors from northern Africa on the Iberian Peninsula, however, had a major influence on both the language and culture of Spain. As the Moors remained in Spain from 711 until 1492, the same year that Columbus "sailed the ocean blue," their influence on the language and culture of Spain was extensive. An example of this is the fact that today the Spanish-speaking world uses the Arabic system of numbers rather than Roman numerals.

Many Arabic words form the basis of terms used today in all Western languages. Examples of these are *alfalfa*, *alcohol*, and *adobe*. The majority, though not all, of the words derived from Arabic begin with *a* or *al*. A common prefix, not beginning in *a* or *al*, is *guadal*, of Arabic origin meaning "water," and is found in a series of place names throughout the world. Spain has its Guadalquivir River, Texas has it Guadalupe River and the Solomon Islands in the Pacific have their Guadalcanal, all places that at one time fell under Spanish, and thus indirectly Arabic, influence.

The Spanish Language in the New World

When the Spanish *conquistadores* arrived in the New World in the 16th century, they found three great indigenous civilizations—the Aztecs and Mayans in Mexico, and the Incas in Peru.

Although these indigenous civilizations were in many ways more advanced than Spain's at the time, certain factors—the Spaniards' advanced weaponry, internal divisions within the indigenous tribes and disease—made it possible for the invaders to conquer them. Following the conquest, the *conquistadores* promptly enslaved the Indians and imposed on them Spain's religion, language and culture.

All living languages change. Thus, from the very beginning of Spain's colonization of the Americas, the language there began to differentiate itself from the Spanish spoken on the Peninsula. The most immediate change, of course, was the incorporation of new words into the language. The colonizers needed names for those things that were unknown in Europe at the time such as *tabaco* (tobacco), *chile* (chili), *hamacas* (hammocks), *canoas* (canoes), *maíz* (corn), and *huracanes* (hurricanes).

Moreover, the indigenous civilizations were widely scattered throughout the Americas and their languages were vastly different. Thus, the Spaniards who colonized one region often borrowed Indian words that differed completely from the words used in other regions. This contributed greatly to the development of linguistic differences between standard Peninsular Spanish and Latin American Spanish as well as to the regional differences within Latin America.

Still another factor in the development of Latin American Spanish was the influence of African languages mainly in the Caribbean area when large numbers of slaves were brought there from Africa. This influence survives today mainly in the area of slang.

Because of the great distance from Spain and the low numbers of immigrants arriving from there, Latin American Spanish continued to evolve rather independently during the 17ᵀᴴ and 18ᵀᴴ centuries. During the 18ᵀᴴ and 19ᵀᴴ centuries, many educated Latin Americans were dismayed at these changes in the language and viewed them as "perversions" and "barbarities" that should be eliminated from the language. The struggle of these linguistic purists most probably helped to preserve many elements of standard peninsular Spanish. However, it is just not possible to legislate language or the use of it. Ultimately it is the people who speak it—with its multitude of variations—who determine what is linguistically acceptable and what is not.

The Latin American Spanish of Today

At no time since the arrival of the Spanish *conquistadores* has a linguistic uniformity existed in Latin America. As a result of innumerable ethnic influences and historic events, the Spanish of Latin

America is a varied and dynamic linguistic entity that reflects the great diversity in the Americas.

In fact, a number of Latin American countries have granted official status to the Indian languages spoken by significant numbers of their populations. In both Peru and Bolivia, for example, the Quechua and Aymara languages have official status along with Spanish.

Even in those Latin American countries that do not recognize as official any language other than Spanish, the Indian languages influence usage. In Venezuela, for example, approximately twenty-five Indian languages are spoken so it is natural that a number of words have made their way into popular usage.

Other language influences in Latin America include the use of English in certain Central American countries. In fact, English is the official language of Belize (formerly British Honduras) and much English is spoken all along the eastern coast of Central America due to the large West Indian population.

The way in which people speak is, to a considerable extent, a matter of class. The more educated Latin Americans are more likely to speak so-called "standard Spanish" while the humbler sectors of the population are likely to speak a type of Spanish peppered with native words and expressions. A possible exception to this is the country of Colombia, which has a reputation for excellent Spanish at all class levels.

There are certain areas in which differences in usage seem to be more extensive. Topping the list, quite naturally, is the area of food. For example, in Mexico a *tortilla* is a thin, flat pancake made of either flour or ground corn. A *tortilla* in Cuba, however, is—as it is in Spain—an omelette. Though in nearly all of the Spanish-speaking world "peanuts" are known as *maní*, they are known in Mexico as *cacahuates*, a word of Indian origin.

Another such area is transportation. There are many different names for city buses, intercity buses, taxis, jitneys, auto parts, etc. For example, a *guagua* in the Caribbean basin is the name for a "bus." In Chile, however, the word is used to mean "baby." To further complicate matters, a city bus in Mexico is known as a *camión*, which is the word used in most parts of the Spanish-speaking world for "truck."

Courteous expressions often differ as well. Especially tricky is knowing whether to address a person formally or familiarly, that is, whether to use the *tú* (familiar) or the *usted* (formal) for "you." Some countries are just more formal than others. The Mexicans, for example, are very formal in contrast, say, to the Cubans who are famous for giving offense where no offense is intended by using *tú* too liberally.

A particularly dangerous area is that of bad language. There are quite a number of words that are perfectly ordinary and correct in one country and downright filthy in another. Every Spanish-speaker has a favorite anecdote based on these treacherous differences.

All these linguistic differences, though not always easy to cope with, are what makes the Spanish of Latin America so interesting. Therefore, they should not be viewed as a negative, but rather as a reflection of a vast and fascinating ethnic diversity.

A BRIEF GUIDE TO SPANISH PRONUNCIATION

This dictionary and phrasebook provides a phonetic pronunciation for all vocabulary and phrases. However, as many English-speaking people have studied Spanish at some time in their lives and as the Spanish sound system is relatively simple, a review of the rules of pronunciation may be all that some people require.

There are, of course, variations in the pronunciation of Spanish from one Latin American country to another. The pronunciation provided in this book is what is considered standard Latin American pronunciation.

Vowels

The pronunciation of the Spanish vowels is much simpler than the pronunciation of English vowels, as each vowel has only one sound. An English vowel, in contrast, can have from five to seven different sounds.

The Spanish vowel sounds are as follows:

A	The sound of <u>a</u> in "father"
E	The sound of <u>a</u> in "date"
I	The sound of <u>ee</u> in "meet"
O	The sound of <u>o</u> in "go"
U	The sound of <u>o</u> in "who"

Diphthongs

A diphthong is a combination of a weak and a strong vowel pronounced together in the same syllable. The following are the more common diphthongs with their pronunciation:

AI	The sound of i in "side"
AU	The sound of ow in "cow"
EI	The sound of ay in "say"
IA	The sound of ya in "yard"
IE	The sound of ye in "yet"
OI	The sound of oy in "boy"

Consonants

Only a limited number of Spanish consonants present problems in pronunciation. The rest are either identical to English or very similar. The following are the ones that require special attention:

B and V	Both are pronounced alike, but each have two different pronunciations depending on where they fall in a word or sentence. B or V at the beginning of a sentence or phrase is pronounced like the B in "bed." B or V between vowels has a soft sound, more like the English V.
C	Sounds like S before E and I. Sounds like K before A, O and U.
G	Sounds like the English H before E and I.
H	Always silent.
J	Similar to the English H.
LL	Like the Y in "yes."
Ñ	Like the NY in "canyon."
Q	Q is always followed by a U in Spanish and is pronounced like the English K.
X	Before a consonant, it sounds like the English S.
	Before a vowel, like the English word "eggs."

Z   Like the English S.

W and K   These letters are not a part of the Spanish alphabet and are only found in certain foreign words.

Stress

In Spanish the stress falls naturally on the next-to-last syllable in words ending in a vowel, *n* or *s*. If a word ends in a consonant other than *n* or *s*, the stress falls on the last syllable. Exceptions to the above rules are indicated by an accent over the stressed syllable.

A BRIEF OVERVIEW OF SPANISH GRAMMAR

The casual traveler to Latin America is not likely to master Spanish grammar in the period immediately before or during the trip. Thus, it is beyond the scope of this book to delve into its complexities. However, it is very useful to have certain notions of its structure. The following outline should be helpful.

Nouns

In Spanish, every noun is either masculine or feminine. Typically nouns ending in *o* are masculine and nouns ending in *a* are feminine. The gender of nouns that end in some other letter simply must be learned. The gender of nouns is indicated by the articles used with them. The definite article "the" in Spanish has four forms, masculine singular *el*, masculine plural *los*, feminine singular *la* and feminine plural *las*.

Singular

el libro	the book
(el LEE-broh)	
la mesa	the table
(lah MAY-say)	

Plural

los libros	the books
(lohs LEE-brohs)	
las mesas	the tables
(lahs MAY-sahs)	

The English articles "a" and "an" are *un* (masculine) and *una* (feminine) in Spanish.

un libro   a book
(oon LEE-broh)

una mesa   a table
(OO-nah MAY-sah)

When *un* is pluralized to *unos* and *una* to *unas*, the meaning is "some."

unos libros   some books
(OO-nohs LEE-brohs)

unas mesas   some tables
(OO-nahs MAY-sahs)

It is very easy to make Spanish nouns plural. The rule is that you add *s* to any noun ending in a vowel and *es* to any noun ending in a consonant.

boleto	ticket	*boletos*	tickets
(boh-LAY-toh)		(boh-LAY-tohs)	
tren	train	*trenes*	trains
(trayn)		(TRAY-nays)	

Adjectives

In Spanish, adjectives—those words that either limit or describe nouns—agree with the nouns they modify in both gender and number. This is somewhat difficult to master but fortunately errors in agreement rarely stand in the way of understanding.

It is important, though, to know that descriptive adjectives usually follow the noun in Spanish rather than precede it as they do in English. So while English-speakers say "red dress," Spanish-speakers will say "dress red," (*vestido rojo*, bays-TEE-doh ROH-hoh).

Possessive adjectives are a special type of adjective that—as the name implies—shows possession. They are the Spanish forms of "our", "my", "his", "their", etc.

Singular		**Plural**	
mi	my	*mis*	my
(mee)		(mees)	
su	his/her/your	*sus*	their/your
(soo)		(soos)	
nuestro	our (m)	*nuestros*	our (m)
(noo-AYS-troh)		(noo-AYS-trohs)	
nuestra	our (f)	*nuestras*	our (f)
(noo-AYS-trah)		(noo-AYS-trahs)	

These adjectives agree with the thing possessed rather than with the possessor. Thus "my books" is not *mi libros*, but rather *mis libros*.

It should be noted that the possession of a noun by another noun is indicated differently in Spanish than it is in English, which uses "'s" or "s'" to show possession. Possession in Spanish is indicated by using the preposition *de* followed by the possessor. So in Spanish, "Alfred's letter" would be "the letter of Alfred," *la carta de Alfredo*. When the article *el* follows the preposition *de*, it contracts to *del*. Therefore, the "taxi door" ("the door of the taxi") becomes *la puerta del taxi*.

Demonstrative adjectives—so called because they demonstrate or point out—are still another special type of adjective. They are the equivalent of our "this," "that," "these" and "those." There are two forms for "that" and "those" in Spanish, one that points out something near the person spoken to and the other, to something distant from both the person speaking and the person spoken to.

These forms are as follows:

MASCULINE FEMININE
Singular

este	*esta*	this (<u>noun</u>) (near
(ESS-tay)	(ESS-tah)	speaker)
ese	*esa*	that (<u>noun</u>) (near
(ESS-say)	(ESS-sah)	person spoken to)
aquel	*aquella*	that (<u>noun</u>) (distant
(ah-KAYL)	(ah-KAY-yah)	from both)

Plural

estos	*estas*	these (<u>noun</u>) (near
(ESS-tohs)	(ESS-tahs)	speaker)
esos	*esas*	those (<u>noun</u>) (near
(ESS-ohs)	(ESS-ahs)	person spoken to)
aquellos	*aquellas*	those (<u>noun</u>)
(ah-KAY-yohs)	(ah-KAY-yahs)	(distant from both)

Pronouns

The pronouns used as the subjects of sentences are as follows:

Singular	Plural		
yo	I	*nosotros/as*	we
(yoh)		(noh-SOH-trohs/trahs)	
tú	you (fam.)		
(too)			
usted	you (for.)	*ustedes*	you (for.)
(oo-STAY)		(oo-STAY-days)	
él	he	*ellos*	they (masc.)
(el)		(AYH-yohs)	
ella	she	*ellas*	they (fem.)
(AY-yah)		(AY-yahs)	

As verbs in Spanish are highly inflected, the verb endings often make it clear who the subject of the sentence is. Therefore, it is not always necessary to use the subject pronouns as it is in English. If there is any confusion as to the subjects, it is always appropriate to use them.

The familiar forms for "you," *tú* (or *vos*, which is used in some parts of Central America and the Cone of South America) and *vosotros* are not included in the following section on verbs. These familiar forms are similar to the words "thee" and " thou," which have fallen out of usage in English. Though their equivalents in Spanish are commonly used, it is much safer for the traveler to use the formal *usted* and *ustedes* forms of "you" so as not to risk giving offense by appearing to be too familiar.

Other types of pronouns include the direct and indirect object pronouns. However, these are quite difficult and can be effectively avoided by simply using nouns. Rather than trying to say, "I bought them for her," just say, "I bought the magazines for Mary."

Verbs

Unquestionably, verbs are the most difficult area of Spanish grammar. The following only covers the most basic tenses of regular verbs—those verbs that follow consistent patterns throughout all tenses—and a few of the most essential irregular verbs.

In Spanish, all infinitives—the equivalent of "to" plus the verb in English as in "to read," "to play," etc.—end in *ar*, *er* or *ir*. The following are examples of regular *ar*, *er*, and *ir* verbs in the present tense:

_ar_ **verbs** (_comprar_)

yo compro (COHM-proh)	I buy
él/ella/usted compra (COHM-prah)	he/she/you buy(s)
nosotros/as compramos (cohm-PRAH-mohs)	we buy
ustedes compran (COHM-prahn)	they/you (plural) buy

_er_ **verbs** (_vender_)

yo vendo (VAYN-doh)	I sell
él/ella/usted vende (VAYN-day)	he/she/you sell(s)
nosotros vendemos (vayn-DAY-mohs)	we sell
ellos/ellas/ustedes venden (VAYN-dayn)	they/you (plural) sell

_ir_ **verbs** (_vivir_)

yo vivo (VEE-voh)	I live
él/ella/usted vive (VEE-vay)	he/she/you live(s)
nosotros/as vivimos (vee-VEE-mohs)	we live
ellos/ellas/ustedes viven (VEE-vayn)	they/you (plural) live

Those verbs that do not follow regular patterns throughout all tenses are called irregular verbs and have to be learned individually. Included here in the present tense are a few of the commonest irregular verbs.

The **verbs** "to be"

There are two verbs "to be" in Spanish, *ser* (sayr) and *estar* (ess-TAHR). *Ser* is used to show a permanent characteristic such as, "Snow is white," or "Manuel is intelligent." Its forms are:

yo soy (sohy)	I am
él/ella/usted es (ess)	he/she is, you are
nosotros/as somos (SOH-mohs)	we are
ellos/ellas/ustedes son (sohn)	they/you (plural) are

The verb *estar* is used in two ways: 1) to indicate the location of someone or something, such as, "Cancún is in Mexico" or "The book is on the table" and 2) to describe a passing condition such as "Mother is very tired" or "Carlos is sick today." Its forms are:

yo estoy (ess-TOHY)	I am
él/ella/usted está (ess-TAH)	he/she is, you are
nosotros/as estamos (ess-TAH-mohs)	we are
ellos/ellas/ustedes están (ess-TAHN)	they/you (plural) are

The **verb** *tener*

Another very useful irregular verb is *tener* which means "to have" in the sense of "to possess." Its present tense forms are as follows:

yo tengo	I have
(TAYN-goh)	
él/ella/usted tiene	he/she has, you have
(tee-AY-nay)	
nosotros/as tenemos	we have
(tay-NAY-mohs)	
ellos/ellas/ustedes tienen	they/you (plural) have
(tee-AY-nayn)	

The verb *ir*, "to go" is particularly useful as the basis for forming a relatively simple substitute for the future tense. Here are its present tense forms:

The **verb** *ir*

yo voy	I go, I'm going
(vohy)	
él/ella/usted va	he/she goes, you go
(vah)	he's/she's/you're going
nosotros/as vamos	we go, we're going
(VAH-mohs)	
ellos/ellas/ustedes van	they/you go,
(vahn)	they're/you're (plural) going

To form the substitute for the future tense, choose the appropriate form of *ir* and follow it with the preposition *a* plus an infinitive.

Van a visitar el museo. They're going to visit the museum.
(Vahn ah vee-see-TAHR el moo-SAY-oh.)
Voy a comer allí mañana. I'm going to eat there tomorrow.
(Vohy ah coh-MAYR ah-EE mah-NYAN-nah.)

Past Tense

There are various verb tenses in Spanish that indicate past actions. However, only the forms of the simple past (or preterite) tense will be included here. This form is used to indicate a one-time action in the past that is over and done with, such as, "I bought a blouse yesterday" or "Juan ate in that restaurant last Sunday."

Here are the simple past tense forms of the regular verbs:

comprar (to buy)

yo compré
(cohm-PRAY)
I bought

él/ella/usted compró
(cohm-PROH)
he/she/you bought

nosotros/as compramos
(cohm-PRAH-mohs)
we bought

ellos/ellas/ustedes compraron
(cohm-PRAH-rohn)
they/you (plural) bought

vender (to sell)

yo vendí
(vayn-DEE)
I sold

él/ella/usted vendió
(vayn-DYOH)
he/she/you sold

nosotros/as vendimos
(vayn-DEE-mohs)
we sold

ellos/ellas/ustedes vendieron
(vayn-dee-YEHR-ohn)
they/you (plural) sold

vivir (to live)

yo viví
(vee-VEE)
I lived

él/ella/usted vivió	he/she/you lived
(vee-VYOH)	
nosotros/as vivimos	we lived
(vee-VEE-mohs)	
ellos/ellas/ustedes vivieron	they/you (plural) lived
(vee-VYEHR-ohn)	

The following are a few of the commonest irregular verbs in the simple past tense:

ser (to be)

yo fui	I was
(fooee)	
él/ella/usted fue	he/she was/you were
(fooay)	
nosotros/as fuimos	we were
(FOOEE-mohs)	
ellos/ellas/ustedes fueron	they/you (plural) were
(FOOYER-ohn)	

ir (to go)

The simple past of *ir* is exactly the same as the simple past of *ser*. Only context makes it clear which verb these forms represent.

estar (to be)

yo estuve	I was
(ess-TOO-vay)	
él/ella/usted estuvo	he/she was, you were
(ess-TOO-voh)	
nosotros/ as estuvimos	we were
(ess-too-VEE-mohs)	
ellos/ellas/ ustedes estuvieron	they/you (plural) were
(ess-too-VEEAYR-ohn)	

tener **(to have)**

yo tuve	I had
(TOO-vay)	
él/ella/usted tuvo	he/she/you had
(TOO-voh)	
nosotros/as tuvimos	we had
(too-VEE-mohs)	
ellos/ellas/ustedes	they/you had
tuvieron	
(too-VEEAY-rohn)	

There are many other verb tenses in Spanish. However, a rudimentary knowledge of the above—simple present, the simple past and substitute for the future—will go a long way in helping the traveler to communicate basic information in Spanish.

Negatives

To make a sentence negative, simply put the word *no* directly before the verb.

"I buy fruit in that store."   *Yo compro fruta en esa tienda.*
(Yoh COHM-proh FROO-tah ayn ESS-ah tee-AYN-dah.)

"I don't buy fruit in   *Yo no compro fruta en* that store."   *esa tienda.*
(Yoh no COHM-proh FROO-tah ayn ESS-ah tee-AYN-dah.)

Questions

There are several ways of forming questions in Spanish. The most usual way is to invert the subject and verb of the sentence.

"You sold the car."	*Usted vendió el carro.*
	(Oo-STAY vayn-DEEOH
	el CAH-roh.)
"Did you sell the car?"	*¿Vendió usted el carro?*
	(¿Vayn-DEEOH
	oo-STAY el CAH-roh?)

Note the inverted question mark at the beginning of the question.

Adverbs

In Spanish, many adverbs end with *mente*. This ending is like the "ly" in English. Thus the word *lentamente* (layn-tah-MAYN-tay) is equivalent to "slowly" in English. There are, however, many other adverbs in Spanish that do not end in *mente* and simply have to be learned as adverbs. For example, another word for "slowly" is *despacio* (days-PAH-see-oh).

Prepositions

These pesky little words tend to be the last forms to be mastered in any foreign language. This is because their use varies so much from one language to another.

For example, in English one speaks "to" someone; in Spanish one speaks "with" someone. In English you get married "to" someone; in Spanish, "with" someone. In English you "take care of"; in Spanish, the concept of "take care of" is contained in the verb *cuidar* and is not followed by a separate preposition.

Though problematic, prepositions will only occasionally lead to misunderstanding.

ABBREVIATIONS

Parts Of Speech And Other Relevant Terms

adjective	adj.
adverb	adv.
article	art.
common usage	com.
conjunction	conj.
familiar	fam.
formal	for.
legal	leg.
medical	med.
noun	n.
plural	plu.
political	pol.
preposition	prep.
pronoun	pron.
singular	sing.
verb	v.

Countries And Regions

Andes	*Andes*
Argentina	*Arg.*
Bolivia	*Bol.*
Caribbean	*Carib.*
Central America	*CA*
Chile	*Chi.*
Colombia	*Col.*
Costa Rica	*CR*
Cuba	*Cuba*
Dominican Republic	*Dom.*
Ecuador	*Ec.*
El Salvador	*Sal.*

Guatemala	*Gua.*
Honduras	*Hon.*
Latin America	*LA*
Nicaragua	*Nic.*
Panama	*Pan.*
Paraguay	*Para.*
Peru	*Pe.*
Puerto Rico	*PR*
River Plate	*RP*
South America	*SA*
Uruguay	*Uru.*
Venezuela	*Ven.*

SPANISH-ENGLISH DICTIONARY

A

a (ah) prep. at; to

abajo (ah-BAH-hoh) adv. below; under; underneath

abarrotes (ah-bah-ROH-tays) n. *Mex.* groceries

abierto (ah-bee-AYR-toh) adj. open

abogado (ah-boh-GAH-doh) n. lawyer

abordo (ah-BORH-doh) on board

abrazo (ah-BRAH-soh) n. embrace

abrigo (ah-BREE-goh) n. coat

abril (ah-BREEL) n. April

abrir (ah-BREER) v. open

absolutamente (ahb-soh-loo-tah-MAYN-tay) adv. absolutely

abuela (ah-BWAY-lah) n. grandmother

abuelo (ah-BWAY-loh) n. grandfather

a casa (ah KAH-sah) adv. home

accidente (ahk-see-DAYN-tay) n. accident

acción (ahk-see-OHN) n. action; (com.) stock certificate

accionista (ahk-see-oh-NEES-tah) n. (com.) stock-holder

aceite (ah-SAY-tay) n. oil

aceituna (ay-say-TOO-nah) n. olive

acelerar (ay-say-lay-RAHR) v. accelerate

acento (ah-SAYN-toh) n. accent

aceptar (ah-sayp-TAHR) v. accept

acera (ah-SAY-rah) n. sidewalk (except *Mex. RP*)

acerca de (ah-SAYR-cah day) prep. about

actividad (ahk-tee-vee-DAHD) n. activity

actor (ahk-TOHR) n. actor

actual (ahk-too-AHL) adj. present

acuerdo (ah-KUAYR-doh) n. agreement

adentro (ah-DAYN-troh) adv. within

adicional (ah-dee-see-oh-NAHL) adj. additional

adiós (ah-dee-OHS) interj. good-bye

admisión (ahd-mee-see-OHN) n. admission

admitir (ahd-mee-TEEHR) v. admit; allow

aduana (ah-DWAH-nah) n. customhouse

aeropuerto (ah-ay-roh-PWAYR-toh) n. airport

afeitar(se) (ah-fay-TAHR-say) v. shave

agencia (ah-HAYN-see-ah) n. agency;
     Chi. pawnshop

agente (ah-HAYN-tay) n. agent

agosto (ah-GOHS-toh) n. August

agua (AH-gwah) n. water

aguamala (ah-gwah-MAH-lah) n. *Carib., Mex.*
     jellyfish

agudo (ah-GOO-doh) adj. sharp

agujero (ah-goo-HAY-roh) n. hole (bored)

ahora (ah-OH-rah) adv. now

ahora mismo (ah-OH-rah MEES-moh) adv.
     right now

ahorrar (ah-oh-RAHR) v. save (money)

aire (AH-ee-ray) n. air

aire acondicionado (AH-ee-ray ah-cohn-dee-see-
     oh-NAH-doh) n. air conditioning

ají (ah-HEE) n. *Cuba, Ven.* bell pepper

ajo (AH-hoh) n. garlic

albaricoque (ahl-bah-ree-COH-kay) n. apricot
     (except *Arg., Mex., Uru.*)

alberca (ahl-BAYR-cah) n. *Mex.* swimming pool

alcohol (ahl-COHL) n. alcohol

alfombra (ahl-FOHM-brah) n. carpet

algo (AHL-goh) pron. something; adv. somewhat

algodón (ahl-goh-DOHN) n. cotton

alguien (AHL-ghee-ayn) pron. someone; anyone

alguno (ahl-GOO-noh) adj. some; any

algunos (ahl-GOO-nohs) pron. some

al lado de (ahl LAH-doh day) prep. beside

almacén (ahl-mah-SAYN) n. warehouse; store; *Arg.* food store; *Mex.* department store

al menos (ahl MAY-nohs) at least

almuerzo (ahl-moo-AYR-soh) n. lunch; midday meal (except *Mex.*)

al por mayor (ahl pohr mah-YOHR) adv. wholesale

alquilar (ahl-key-LAHR) v. rent

alto (AHL-toh) adj. tall; high

altura (ahl-TOO-rah) n. altitude; height

allí (ah-EE) adv. over there

allí mismo (ah-EE MEES-moh) adv. right there

amar (ah-MAHR) v. love

amarillo (ah-mah-REE-yoh) n., adj. yellow

ámbar (AHM-bahr) n. amber

ambulancia (ahm-boo-LAHN-see-ah) n. ambulance

a menos que (ah MAY-nohs kay) conj. unless

amigo(a) (ah-MEE-goh/gah) n. friend

amor (ah-MOHR) n. love

ananá (ah-nah-NAH) n. *Arg.* pineapple

ancho (AHN-choh) adj. broad; wide

ante (AHN-tay) prep. before

antes de que (AHN-tays day kay) conj. before

anteojos (ahn-tay-OH-hohs) n. *RP* eyeglasses

antigüedad (ahn-tee-gway-DAHD) n. antique

antiguo (ahn-TEE-gwoh) adj. ancient

anual (ah-noo-AHL) adj. annual

anunciar (ah-noon-see-AHR) v. announce; advertise

anuncio comercial (ah-NOON-see-oh coh-mayr-see-AHL) n. advertisement

año (AHN-yoh) n. year

apagar (ah-pah-GAHR) v. put out; turn off

apartamento (ah-pahr-tah-MAYN-toh) n. apartment (except *Mex.*)

aparte (ah-PAHR-tay) adv. apart

apellido (ah-pay-YEE-doh) n. last name

aprender (ah-prayn-DAYR) v. learn

aquí (ah-KEY) adv. here

archivar (ahr-chee-VAHR) v. file

archivo (ahr-CHEE-voh) n. archives; file

área (AH-ray-ah) n. area

aretes (ah-RAY-tays) n. *Cuba, Mex.* earrings

arma (AHR-mah) n. weapon

aros (AH-rohs) n. *Arg., Chi.* earrings

arreglar (ah-ray-GLAHR) v. arrange; fix

arroz (ah-ROHS) n. rice

arte (AHR-tay) n. art

artículo (ahr-TEE-coo-loh) n. article

artista (ahr-TEES-tah) n. artist; entertainer

asado (ah-SAH-doh) adj. roasted; n. *RP* steak; barbecue

ascensor (ah-sayn-SOHR) n. *Arg., Ecu., Pe., Uru., Ven.* elevator

asegurar (ah-say-goo-RAHR) v. secure; insure

asiento (ah-see-AYN-toh) n. seat

asistente (ah-sees-TAYN-tay) n. assistant

asistir (ah-sees-TEER) v. attend

aterrizaje (ah-tay-ree-SAH-hay) n. landing

a través de (ah trah-VAYS day) prep. through; across

aumentar (ah-oo-mayn-TAHR) v. increase

aún (ah-OON) adv. still; yet

aunque (ah-OON-kay) conj. although

auto (AH-oo-toh) n. car

autobus (AH-oo-toh-boos) n. *Ven.* city bus; *Arg., Chi., Cuba, Mex.* intercity bus

automático (ah-oo-toh-MAH-tee-coh) adj. automatic

avance (ah-VAHN-say) n. advance payment

avanzar (ah-vahn-SAHR) v. advance

a veces (ah VAY-says) adv. sometimes

avenida (ah-vay-NEE-dah) n. avenue

avión (ah-vee-OHN) n. airplane

ayer (ah-YAYR) adv. yesterday

ayuda (ah-YOO-dah) n. help

ayudar (ah-yoo-DAHR) v. help

azúcar (ah-SOO-cahr) n. sugar

azulejo (ah-soo-LAY-hoh) n. glazed tile

B

bailar (bah-ee-LAHR) v. dance

bajar (bah-HAR) v. go down

banco (BAHN-coh) n. bench; bank

bandera (bahn-DAY-rah) n. flag

banqueta (bahn-KAY-tah) n. *Mex.* sidewalk

bañadera (bah-nyah-DAY-rah) n. *Arg., Cuba* bathtub

bañar (bah-NYAHR) v. bathe

bañar(se) (bah-NYAHR-say) v. take a bath

bañera (bah-NYAY-rah) n. *PR, Uru., Ven.* bathtub

baño (BAH-nyoh) n. bath; bathroom

bar (bahr) n. bar

barata (bah-RAH-tah) n. *Mex.* sale

barato (bah-RAH-toh) adj. cheap

barbero (bahr-BAY-roh) n. barber

barco (BAHR-coh) n. boat

base (BAH-say) n. base; basis; *Mex.* permanent; wave

bastante (bahs-TAHN-tay) adv. enough

basura (bah-SOO-rah) n. garbage

batería (bah-tay-REE-ah) n. battery (car)

baúl (bah-OOL) n. trunk

beber (bay-BAYR) v. drink

bebé (bay-BAY) n. baby

bebida (bay-BEE-dah) n. drink; beverage

bello (BAY-yoh) adj. beautiful; handsome

besar (bay-SAHR) v. kiss

beso (BAY-soh) n. kiss

betabel (bay-tah-BAYL) n. *Mex.* beet

biblioteca (beeb-lee-oh-TAY-cah) n. library

bicicleta (bee-cee-CLAY-tah) n. bicycle

bicho (BEE-choh) n. insect; small animal; *Cuba* shrewd operator; *PR* (vulgar)

bien (bee-AYN) adv. well; very

bien cocido (bee-AYN coh-SEE-doh) adj. well done (meat)

¡Bienvenido! (bee-ayn-vay-NEE-doh) interj. Welcome!

bife (BEE-fay) n. *RP* steak

biftec (beef-TAYK) n. beefsteak

billete (bee-YAY-tay) n. bill (money)

billetera (bee-yay-TAY-rah) n. *Bol., Chi., Cuba, Ec., Pe.* wallet

bistec (bees-TAYK) n. *Cuba, Mex., Pe.* beefsteak

bizcocho (bees-COH-choh) n. *Cuba* ladyfinger; PR cake, *Mex.* (vulgar)

blanco (BLAHN-coh) n., adj. white

blanquillo (blahn-KEY-yoh) n. *Gua., Mex.* egg (euphemism for *huevo*, which has a double meaning)

blusa (BLOO-sah) n. blouse

boca (BOH-cah) n. mouth

bocaditos (boh-cah-DEE-tohs) n. *Cuba* little sandwiches; *Pe.* snacks

bodega (boh-DAY-gah) n. store; warehouse; *Cuba, Pe., PR, Ven.* grocery store

boga (BOH-gah) n. *Arg.* attorney

bolero (boh-LAY-roh) n. *Mex.* shoeshine boy

boleto (boh-LAY-toh) n. ticket

bolsa (BOHL-sah) n. bag; stock market; *Mex.* purse; *Ec., Pe., Uru.* shopping bag

bombilla (bohm-BEE-yah) n. light bulb (except *Mex.*)

bondadoso (bohn-dah-DOH-soh) adj. kind

bonito (boh-NEE-toh) adj. pretty

borrar (boh-RAHR) v. erase

botana (boh-TAH-nah) n. *Mex.* snack

botella (boh-TAY-yah) n. bottle

botica (boh-TEE-cah) n. *Carib.* drug store

botón (boh-TOHN) n. button

botones (boh-TOH-nays) n. bellboy

brazalete (brah-sah-LAY-tay) n. bracelet

brazo (BRAH-soh) n. arm

breve (BRAY-vay) adj. brief

broma (BROH-mah) n. joke

brujería (broo-hay-REE-ah) n. witchcraft

bueno (BWAY-noh) adj. good

bufete (boo-FAY-tay) n. *Mex.* law office

buscar (boos-CAHR) v. look for

C

caballero (cah-bah-YAY-roh) n. gentleman

caballo (cah-BAH-yoh) n. horse

cabello (cah-BAY-yoh) n. hair

cabeza (cah-BAY-sah) n. head

cacahuates (cah-cah-oo-AH-tays) n. *Mex.* peanuts

cada (CAH-dah) adj. each; every

cada uno (CAH-dah OO-noh) pron. every one

café (cah-FAY) n. coffee; café; n., adj. *Mex.* brown

caja (CAH-hah) n. box; safe; cashier's window

caja de seguridad (CAH-hah day say-goo-ree-
DAHD) n. safe-deposit box

cajero (cah-HAY-roh) n. cashier; teller

cajón (cah-HON) n. drawer

calcetín (cahl-say-TEEN) n. sock

calefacción (cah-lah-fahk-see-OHN) n. central
heating

calendario (cah-layn-DAH-ree-oh) n. calendar

calentura (cah-layn-TOO-rah) n. *Mex.* fever

calidad (cah-lee-DAHD) n. quality

caliente (cah-lee-AYN-tay) adj. hot

calor (cah-LOHR) n. heat

calle (CAH-yay) n. street

cama (CAH-mah) n. bed

cámara (CAH-mah-rah) n. camera; chamber

camarero (cah-mah-RAY-roh) n. waiter

camarón (cah-mah-ROHN) n. shrimp

cambiar (cahm-bee-AHR) v. change; exchange

cambio (CAHM-bee-oh) n. change; exchange

cambur (cahm-BOOR) n. *Ven.* banana

caminar (cah-mee-NAHR) v. walk

camino (cah-MEE-noh) n. road

camión (cah-mee-OHN) n. truck; *Mex.* city bus

camisa (cah-MEE-sah) n. shirt

campamento (cahm-pah-MAYN-toh) n. camp

campo (CAHM-poh) n. country (rural area)

canasta (cah-NAHS-tah) n. basket

canción (cahn-see-OHN) n. song

canela (cah-NAY-lah) n. cinnamon

cansado (cahn-SAH-doh) adj. tired

cantante (cahn-TAHN-tay) n. singer

cantar (cahn-TAHR) v. sing

cantidad (cahn-tee-DAHD) n. amount

cañón (cah-NYOHN) n. canyon

capital (cah-pee-TAHL) n. capital

cara (CAH-rah) n. face

carburador (cahr-boo-rah-DOHR) n. carburetor

cárcel (CAHR-sayl) n. jail

carga (CAHR-gah) n. freight; cargo

cargamento (cahr-gah-MAYN-toh) n. load; shipment

carne (CAHR-nay) n. meat

carne de puerco (CAHR-nay day PWAYR-coh) n. pork

carne de res (CAHR-nay day rays) n. beef

carnet de manejar (cahr-NAYT day mah-nay-HAHR) n. *Chi.* driver's license

caro (CAH-roh) adj. expensive

carreta (cah-RAY-tah) n. cart

carretera (cah-ray-TAY-rah) n. highway

carro (CAH-roh) n. car

carta (CAHR-tah) n. letter

casa (CAH-sah) n. house; home

casaca (cah-SAH-cah) n. *Pe.* jacket

casa de correos (CAH-sayh day coh-RAY-ohs) n. post office (except *Mex.*)

casado (cah-SAH-doh) adj. married

casi (CAH-see) adv. almost

caso (CAH-soh) n. case

catedral (cah-tay-DRAHL) n. cathedral

causa (CAH-oo-sah) n. cause; lawsuit

causar (cah-oo-SAHR) v. cause

cazar (cah-SAHR) v. hunt

cebolla (say-BOH-yah) n. onion

cédula de identidad (SAY-doo-lah day ee-dayn-tee-DAHD) n. *Bol., Ec., Mex., Pe., RP* ID card

centavo (sayn-TAH-voh) n. cent

central (sayn-TRAHL) adj. central

cepillo de dientes (say-PEE-yoh day dee-AYN-tays) n. toothbrush

cerámica (say-RAH-mee-cah) n. ceramics

cerca (SAYR-cah) adv. near

cerillo (say-REE-yoh) n. *CA, Mex.* match

cero (SAY-roh) n. zero

cerrar (say-RAHR) v. close

certificado (sayr-tee-fee-CAH-doh) n. certificate

cerveza (sayr-VAY-sah) n. beer

chabacano (chah-bah-CAH-noh) n. *Mex.* apricot

chamaco (chah-MAH-coh) n. *Mex.* boy; kid

chamarra (chah-MAH-rah) n. *Mex.* jacket

champaña (chahm-PAH-nyah) n. champagne

champú (chahm-POO) n. shampoo

chaqueta (chah-KAY-tah) n. jacket

chauchas (CHAH-oo-chahs) n. *RP* green beans

cheque (CHAY-kay) n. check

chicle (CHEE-clay) n. chewing gum

chico (CHEE-coh) n. kid; adj. small

chile (CHEE-lay) n. chilli pepper

chiste (CHEE-stay) n. joke

chocar (choh-CAHR) v. collide

chocolate (choh-coh-LAH-tay) n. chocolate

chofer (choh-FAYR) n. driver

chorizo (choh-REE-soh) n. salami-type sausage

chuleta (choo-LAY-tah) n. chop; cutlet

cielo (see-AY-loh) n. sky; heaven

cien (see-AYN) n., adj. one hundred

ciento (see-AYN-toh) n., adj. one hundred

cierre (see-AY-ray) n. *Mex. Uru.* zipper

cigarrillo (see-gah-REE-yoh) n. *Ec., Pan., Pe., RP* cigarette

cigarro (see-GAH-roh) n. cigarette; *Ec., PR*, cigar

cinco (SEEN-coh) n., adj. five

cincuenta (seen-KWAYN-tah) n., adj. fifty

cinturón (seen-too-ROHN) n. belt

círculo (SEER-coo-loh) n. circle

cita (SEE-tah) n. appointment; date

ciudad (see-oo-DAHD) n. city

ciudadano (see-oo-da-DAH-noh) n. citizen

clase (KLAH-say) n. class; kind

cliente (clee-AYN-tay) n. customer; client

clima (KLEE-mah) n. climate; *Mex.* air conditioning

cobija (coh-BEE-hah) n. *Mex.* blanket

cocina (coh-SEE-nah) n. kitchen; stove

cocinar (coh-see-NAHR) v. cook

coche (COH-chay) n. car

cochera (coh-CHAY-rah) n. *Mex.* garage

colectivo (coh-layk-TEE-voh) n. *Arg., Bol.* city bus; adj. collective

colgador (cohl-gah-DOHR) n. clothes hanger

color (coh-LOHR) n. color

comedor (coh-may-DORH) n. dining room

comenzar (coh-mayn-SAHR) v. begin

comer (coh-MAYR) v. eat

comercial (coh-mayr-see-AHL) adj. commercial

cómico (COH-mee-coh) n. comedian; adj. funny

comercio (coh-MAYR-see-oh) n. business

comida (coh-MEE-dah) n. food; meal

comisión (coh-mee-see-OHN) n. commission

como (COH-moh) adv. as; like; conj. as; when; if; so that

¿cómo? (COH-moh) adv. how?

cómodo (COH-moh-doh) adj. comfortable

compañero (cohm-pah-NYAY-roh) n. companion; partner

compañía (cohm-pah-NYEE-ah) n. company

compartir (cohm-pahr-TEER) v. share

compinche (cohm-PEEN-chay) n. *Bol., RP* buddy

completo (cohm-PLAY-toh) adj. complete

comprador (cohm-prah-DOHR) n. buyer

comprar (cohm-PRAHR) v. buy

comprender (cohm-prayn-DAYR) v. understand

computadora (cohm-poo-tah-DOH-rah) n. computer

con (cohn) prep. with

concierto (cohn-see-AYR-toh) n. concert

conclusión (cohn-cloo-see-OHN) n. conclusion

condición (cohn-dee-see-OHN) n. condition

conducir (cohn-doo-SEER) v. drive

conferencia (cohn-fay-RAYN-see-ah) n. lecture

confiar (cohn-fee-AHR) v. trust

congreso (cohn-GRAY-soh) n. congress; convention

conocer (coh-noh-SAYR) v. know; be acquainted with

conocimiento (coh-noh-see-mee-AYN-toh) n. knowledge

consejo (cohn-SAY-hoh) n. advice

considerado (cohn-see-day-RAH-doh) adj. considerate

consignación (cohn-seeg-nah-see-OHN) n. consignment

constituir (cohn-stee-too-EER) v. constitute

construcción (cohn-strook-see-OHN) n. construction

consulado (cohn-soo-LAH-doh) n. consulate

consultar (cohn-sool-TAHR) v. consult

consultorio (cohn-sool-TOH-ree-oh) n. doctor's office

contacto (cohn-TAHK-toh) n. contact; *Mex.* (elec.) outlet

contador (cohn-tah-DOHR) n. accountant

contar (cohn-TAHR) v. count

contener (cohn-tay-NAYR) v. contain

contenido (cohn-tay-NEE-doh) n. content

contestar (cohn-tays-TAHR) v. answer

continuar (cohn-tee-noo-AHR) v. continue

contra (COHN-trah) prep. against

contrato (cohn-TRAH-toh) n. contract

contribuir (cohn-tree-boo-EER) v. contribute

conveniente (cohn-vay-nee-AYN-tay) adj. convenient

conversar (cohn-vayr-SAHR) v. converse

coñac (coh-NYAK) n. cognac; brandy

copa (COH-pah) n. wineglass; *Mex.* drink (alcoholic)

copiar (coh-pee-AHR) v. copy

corazón (coh-rah-SOHN) n. heart

corbata (cohr-BAH-tah) n. necktie

corporación (cohr-poh-rah-see-OHN) n. corporation

correcto (coh-RAYK-toh) adj. correct

corredor (coh-ray-DOHR) n. runner; corridor

corredor de bolsa (coh-ray-DOHR day BOHL-sah) n. stockbrocker

correo (coh-RAY-oh) n. mail; post office

correr (coh-RAYR) v. run

cortar (cohr-TAHR) v. cut

cortina (cohr-TEE-nah) n. curtain

corto (COHR-toh) adj. short

cosa (COH-sah) n. thing

crédito (CRAY-dee-toh) n. credit

creer (cray-AYR) v. believe

criada (cree-AH-dah) n. maid

criado (cree-AH-doh) n. servant

crimen (CREE-mayn) n. crime

cuadra (KWAH-drah) n. city block

cuadro (KWAH-droh) n. square; picture

cualquiera (kwal-key-AY-rah) pron. whichever; whoever

cualquier cosa (kwayl-key-AYR COH-sah) pron. anything

cuando (KWAN-doh) adv. when

¿cuántos? (KWAN-tohs) adj., pron. how many?

cuarenta (kwah-RAYN-tah) n., adj. forty

cuarto (KWAHR-toh) adj. fourth; n. quarter; room

cuarto de dormir (KWAHR-toh day dohr-MEER) n. bedroom

cuate (KWAH-tay) n. *Mex.* twin; buddy

cuatro (KWAH-troh) n., adj. four

cubrir (coo-BREER) v. cover

cuchara (coo-CHAH-rah) n. spoon

cuchillito de afeitar (coo-chee-YEE-toh day ah-fay-TAHR) n. *Cuba* razor blade

cuchillo (coo-CHEE-yoh) n. knife

cuello (coo-AY-yoh) n. neck; collar

cuenta (coo-AYN-tah) n. account; bill

cuero (coo-AY-roh) n. leather

cuerpo (coo-AYR-poh) n. body

cueva (coo-AY-vah) n. cave

¡Cuidado! (coo-ee-DAH-doh) imper. Be careful!

cuidar (coo-ee-DAHR) v. take care of

cultura (cool-TOO-rah) n. culture

cumpleaños (coom-play-AH-nyohs) n. birthday

cuneta (coo-NAY-tah) n. *Chi.* sidewalk

cura (COO-rah) n. cure; priest

curar (coo-RAHR) v. treat; cure

D

dañar (dah-NYAHR) v. hurt

daño (DAH-nyoh) n. damage

dar (dahr) v. give

dar(se) cuenta de (DAHR-say coo-AYN-tah day) v. realize

dar(se) prisa (DAHR-say PREE-sah) v. hurry

de (day) prep. of; from; about

deber (day-BAYR) n. duty; v. owe; ought to; must; should

débil (DAY-beel) adj. weak

decir (day-SEER) v. say; tell

decisión (day-see-see-OHN) n. decision

declaración (day-clah-rah-see-OHN) n. declaration; statement

declarar (de-clah-RAHR) v. declare

dedo (DAY-doh) n. finger

dedo del pie (DAY-doh del pee-AY) n. toe

delgado (dayl-GAH-doh) adj. thin

delicioso (day-lee-see-OH-soh) adj. delicious

demanda (day-MAHN-dah) n. demand; lawsuit

demandar (day-mahn-DAHR) v. demand; sue

demasiado (day-mah-see-AH-doh) adj; pron. too much

demostrar (day-moh-STRAHR) v. demonstrate

dentista (dayn-TEE-stah) n. dentist

departamento (day-pahr-tah-MAYN-toh) n. department; *Mex.* apartment

dependiente (day-payn-dee-AYN-tay) n. clerk; adj. dependent

deporte (day-POHR-tay) n. sport

depositar (day-poh-see-TAHR) v. deposit

deposito (day-POH-see-toh) n. deposit

derecho (day-RAY-choh) n. right; law; adj. right; straight; adv. straight ahead

de repente (day ray-PAYN-tay) adv. suddenly

desagradable (day-sah-grah-DAH-blay) adj. disagreeable

desayuno (day-sah-YOO-noh) n. breakfast

descansar (days-cahn-SAHR) v. rest

describir (days-cree-VEER) v. discover

descripción (days-creep-see-OHN) n. description

descubrir (days-coo-VREER) v. describe

descuento (days-coo-AYN-toh) n. discount

desde (DAYS-day) prep. from; since

desear (day-say-AHR) v. desire; want

desocupado (day-soh-coo-PAH-doh) adj. unoccupied

despacio (days-PAH-see-oh) adv. slowly

despertador (days-payr-tah-DOHR) n. alarm clock

después (days-poo-AYS) adv. after; afterwards

detalle (day-TAH-yay) n. detail

detener (day-tay-NAYR) v. stop

determinar (day-tayr-mee-NAHR) v. determine

detrás (day-TRAHS) adv. behind

deuda (DAY-oo-dah) n. debt

de vez en cuando (day vays ayn KWAN-doh) adv. once in a while

devolver (day-vohl-VAYR) v. return; give back

día (DEE-ah) n. day

día festivo (DEE-ah fay-STEE-voh) n. holiday

día laborable (DEE-ah lah-boh-RAH-blay) n. workday

diamante (dee-ah-MAHN-tay) n. diamond

diario (dee-AH-ree-oh) n. daily paper; adj. daily

diciembre (dee-see-AYM-bray) n. December

diente (dee-AYN-tay) n. tooth

diez (dee-AYS) n., adj. ten

diez y nueve (dee-AYS ee noo-AY-vay) n., adj. nineteen

diez y ocho (dee-AYS ee OH-choh) n., adj. eighteen

diferencia (dee-fay-RAYN-see-ah) n. difference

diferente (dee-fay-RAYN-tay) adj. different

difícil (dee-FEE-seel) adj. difficult

dinero (dee-NAY-roh) n. money

dios (dee-OHS) n. god

dirección (dee-rayk-see-OHN) n. direction; address

directo (dee-RAYK-toh) adj. direct

director (dee-rayk-TOHR) n. director; manager

dirigente (dee-ree-HAYN-tay) n. leader

dirigir (dee-ree-HEER) v. direct; manage

discurso (dees-COOR-soh) n. speech

discutir (dees-coo-TEER) v. argue

disponible (dees-poh-NEE-blay) adj. available

distancia (dees-TAHN-see-ah) n. distance

distante (dees-TAHN-tay) adj. distant

distribuir (dees-tree-boo-EER) v. distribute

diversión (dee-vayr-see-OHN) n. recreation

divertido (dee-vayr-TEE-doh) adj. amusing

divertir (dee-vayr-TEER) v. amuse

divertir(se) (dee-vayr-TEER-say) v. have a good time

división (dee-vee-see-OHN) n. division

doble (DOH-blay) adj. double

doce (DOH-say) n., adj. twelve

docena (doh-SAY-nah) n. dozen

doctor (dohk-TOHR) n. doctor

dólar (DOH-lahr) n. dollar

dolor (doh-LOHR) n. pain

dolor de cabeza (doh-LOHR day cah-BAY-sah) n. headache

dolor de estómago (doh-LOHR day ays-TOH-mah-goh) n. stomachache

dolor de muela (doh-LOHR day moo-AY-lah) n. toothache

domingo (doh-MEEN-goh) n. Sunday

¿dónde? (DOHN-day) adv. where?

dormir (dohr-MEER) v. sleep

dormitorio (dohr-mee-TOHR-ee-oh) n. *Bol., Ec., Pe.* bedroom

dos (dohs) n., adj. two

dos veces (dohs VAY-says) adv. twice

drama (DRAH-mah) n. drama; play

droga (DROH-gah) n. drug

ducha (DOO-chah) n. *Cuba, Pe., PR* shower

dueño (doo-AY-nyoh) n. owner

dulce (DOOL-say) adj. sweet; *Pan.* cake

dulces (DOOL-says) n. candy

durante (doo-RAHN-tay) prep. during

durazno (doo-RAHS-noh) n. *Arg., CA, Mex., Pan., Pe.* peach

duro (DOO-roh) adj. hard

E

economía (ay-coh-noh-MEE-ah) n. economy

echar al correo (ay-CHAHR ahl coh-RAY-oh) v. mail

edad (ay-DAHD) n. age

efectivo (ay-fayk-TEE-voh) n. cash; adj. effective

eficiente (ay-fee-see-AYN-tay) adj. efficient

ejemplo (ay-HAYM-ploh) n. example

ejotes (ay-HOH-tays) n. *Mex.* green beans

el (ayl) masc. art. the

él (ayl) pron. he

elemento (ay-lay-MAYN-toh) n. element

elevador (ay-lay-vah-DOHR) n. *Carib., Mex.* elevator

ella (AY-yah) pron. she

ellos (AY-yohs) pron. they

embajada (aym-bah-HAH-dah) n. embassy

embajador (ayn-bah-hah-DOHR) n. ambassador

emparedado (aym-pah-ray-DAH-doh) n. *Bol.* sandwich

empate (aym-PAH-tay) n. *Ven.* girlfriend

empezar (aym-pay-SAHR) v. begin

empleada (aym-lay-AH-dah) n. *Bol., Ec., Uru., Pan.* maid

emplear (aym-play-AHR) v. employ; use

empleo (aym-PLAY-oh) n. job

empresa (aym-PRAY-sah) n. company

empujar (aym-poo-HAHR) v. push

en (ayn) prep. in; on

encaje (ayn-CAH-hay) n. lace

en casa (ayn CAH-sah) adv. at home

encender (ayn-sayn-DAYR) v. light

encontrar (ayn-cohn-TRAHR) v. find; meet

en el extranjero (ayn ayl ays-trahn-HAY-roh) adv. abroad

enero (ay-NAY-roh) n. January

enfermo (ayn-FAYR-moh) adj. sick

engañar (ayn-gahn-YAHR) v. deceive; cheat

ensalada (ayn-sah-LAH-dah) n. salad

en seguida (ayn say-GHEE-dah) adv. at once

enseñar (ayn-say-NYAHR) v. teach

entendimiento (ayn-tayn-dee-mee-AYN-toh) n. understanding

entero (ayn-TAY-roh) adj. entire

en todas partes (ayn TOH-dahs PAHR-tays) adv. everywhere

entonces (ayn-TOHN-says) adv. then

entrada (ayn-TRAH-dah) n. entrance; *Bol.* ticket

entrar (ayn-TRAHR) v. enter; come in

entre (AYN-tray) prep. between; among

entregar (ayn-tray-GAHR) v. deliver

entremeses (ayn-tray-MAY-says) n. hors d'oeuvres

envase (ayn-VAH-say) n. container

en vez de (ayn vays day) prep. instead of

enviar (ayn-vee-AHR) v. send

equipaje (ay-key-PAH-hay) n. luggage

equipo (ay-KEY-poh) n. equipment; team

equivalente (ay-key-vah-LAYN-tay) n., adj. equivalent

equivocado (ay-key-voh-CAH-doh) adj. wrong; mistaken

equivocar(se) (ay-key-voh-CAHR-say) v. make a mistake

error (ay-ROHR) n. mistake

escalera (ays-cah-LAY-rah) n. stairs

escoger (ays-coh-HAYR) v. choose

esconder (ays-cohn-DAYR) v. hide

escribir (ays-cree-VEER) v. write

escritor (ays-cree-TOHR) n. writer

escuchar (ays-coo-CHAHR) v. listen to

escuela (ays-KWAY-lah) n. school

escultor (ays-cool-TOHR) n. sculptor

esmeralda (ays-may-RAHL-dah) n. emerald

estancia (ays-TAHN-see-ah) n. *RP* farm

¡Eso es! (AY-soh ays) interj. That's it!

especial (ays-pay-see-AHL) adj. special

espejuelos (ays-pay-HWAY-lohs) n. *Cuba* eyeglasses

esperar (ays-pay-RAHR) v. wait for; hope for; expect

espinacas (ays-pee-NAH-cahs) n. spinach

esposa (ays-POH-sah) n. wife

esposo (ays-POH-soh) n. husband

esquina (ays-KEY-nah) n. corner

establecer (ays-tah-blay-SAYR) v. establish

estación (ays-tah-see-OHN) n. station; season

estacionamiento (ays-tah-see-oh-nah-mee-AYN-toh) n. *Mex., Uru.* parking lot

estado de cuentas (ays-TAH-doh day coo-AYN-tahs) n. (com.) statement

estampilla (ays-tahm-PEE-yah) n. *Bol., Ec., Mex., PR* postage stamp

esta noche (AYS-tah NOH-chay) adv. tonight

estar (ays-TAHR) v. be

estatua (ays-TAH-too-ah) n. statue

este (AYS-tay) n. east; adj. this

estómago (ays-TOH-mah-goh) n. stomach

estudiante (ays-too-dee-AHN-tay) n. student

estudiar (ays-too-dee-AHR) v. study

etiqueta (ay-tee-KAY-tah) n. tag; label

evidente (ay-vee-DAYN-tay) adj. evident

evitar (ay-vee-TAHR) v. avoid

examen (ex-AH-mayn) n. examination

examinar (ex-ah-mee-NAHR) v. examine

exceso (ex-SAY-soh) n. excess

exclusivo (ex-kloo-SEE-voh) adj. exclusive

excursión (ex-coor-see-OHN) n. excursion

exhibición (ex-ee-bee-see-OHN) n. exhibit

éxito (EX-ee-toh) n. success

explicación (ex-plee-cah-see-OHN) n. explanation

explicar (ex-plee-CAHR) v. explain

exportación (ex-pohr-tah-see-OHN) n. export

exportar (ex-pohr-TAHR) v. export

exterior (ex-tay-ree-OHR) adj. exterior; foreign

extranjero (ex-trahn-HAY-roh) n. foreigner; adj. foreign

F

fácil (FAH-seel) adj. easy

fácilmente (FAH-seel-mayn-tay) adv. easily

falda (FAHL-dah) n. skirt; *Cuba* cut of beef

falta (FAHL-tah) n. lack

faltar (fahl-TAHR) v. lack; be absent

familia (fah-MEE-lee-ah) n. family

famoso (fah-MOH-soh) adj. famous

fantástico (fahn-TAHS-tee-coh) adj. fantastic

farmacia (fahr-MAH-see-ah) n. drugstore

febrero (fay-BRAY-roh) n. February

fecha (FAY-chah) n. date

felicitaciones (fay-lee-see-tah-see-OH-nays) n. congratulations

feliz (fay-LEES) adj. happy

feo (FAY-oh) adj. ugly; adv. *Arg., Col., Mex.* bad

ferretería (fay-ray-tay-REE-ah) n. hardware store

ferrocarril (fay-roh-cah-REEL) n. railroad

fiebre (fee-AY-bray) n. fever

fiesta (fee-AY-stah) n. party

finanza (fee-NAHN-sah) n. finance

finca (FEEN-cah) n. *Cuba* farm

fin de semana (feen day say-MAH-nah) n. weekend

fino (FEE-noh) adj. fine; refined

firma (FEER-mah) n. signature

firmar (feer-MAHR) v. sign

flojo (FLOH-hoh) adj. loose; *Mex., Ven.* lazy

foco (FOH-coh) n. focus; *Mex.* light bulb

fondo (FOHN-doh) n. bottom; rear

forma (FOHR-mah) n. form; shape

formar (fohr-MAHR) v. form; shape

fósforo (FOHS-foh-roh) n. match

foto (FOH-toh) n. photo

fracasar (frah-cah-SAHR) v. fail

fracaso (frah-CAH-soh) n. failure

frazada (frah-SAH-dah) n. blanket

frecuentemente (fray-kwayn-tay-MAYN-tay) adv. frequently

fresa (FRAY-sah) n. strawberry

fresco (FRAYS-coh) adj. fresh; cool

frijoles (free-HOH-lays) n. *Carib., Mex.* dry beans

frío (FREE-oh) n., adj. cold

frontera (frohn-TAY-rah) n. border

fruta (FROO-tah) n. fruit

fuera (FWAY-rah) adv. out; outside

fuerte (FWAYR-tay) adj. strong; loud

fumar (foo-MAHR) v. smoke

función (foon-see-OHN) n. function; performance

fusil (foo-SEEL) n. gun; rifle

fútbol (FOOT-bohl) n. soccer

fútbol americano (FOOT-bohl ah-may-ree-CAH-noh) n. football

G

galón (gah-LOHN) n. gallon

galleta (gah-YAY-tah) n. cracker; *Mex.* (also cookie)

ganancias (gah-NAHN-see-ahs) n. profit; *Gua., Mex.* bonus

ganar (gah-NAHR) v. win; earn

gancho (GAHN-choh) n. hook; *Mex.* hanger

ganga (GAHN-gah) n. bargain

garaje (gah-RAH-hay) n. garage

garantía (gah-rahn-TEE-ah) n. guaranty; warranty

garantizar (gah-rahn-tee-SAHR) v. guarantee

garganta (gahr-GAHN-tah) n. throat

gaseosa (gah-say-OH-sah) n. carbonated soft drink

gasolina (gah-soh-LEE-nah) n. gasoline

gastar (gah-STAHR) v. spend

gasto (GAH-stoh) n. expense

gato (GAH-toh) n. cat

general (hay-nay-RAHL) n. adj. general

gente (HAYN-tay) n. people

genuino (hay-noo-EE-noh) adj. genuine

gerencia (hay-RAYN-see-ah) n. management

gerente (hay-RAYN-tay) n. manager

gimnasio (heem-NAH-see-oh) n. gym

ginebra (hee-NAY-brah) n. gin

giro (HEE-roh) n. money order

gobernador (goh-bayr-nah-DOHR) n. governor

gobierno (goh-bee-AYR-noh) n. government

golf (golf) n. golf

golfo (GOHL-foh) n. gulf

goma (GOH-mah) n. rubber; *Cuba* tire; eraser; *Cuba, Ec., Uru.* glue

gordo (GOHR-doh) adj. fat; n. *Mex.* (term of affection)

gracias (GRAH-see-ahs) n. thanks

gran (grahn) adj. large; great

grande (GRAHN-day) adj. large; great

granja (GRAHN-hah) n. farm

gratis (GRAH-tees) adv. free (at no cost)

gripa (GREE-pah) n. *Mex.* flu

gripe (GREE-pay) n. flu

gris (grees) adj. gray

gritar (gree-TAHR) v. shout

grupo (GROO-poh) n. group

guagua (GWAH-gwah) n. *Chi.* baby; *Cuba* bus

guajiro (gwah-HEE-roh) n. *Cuba* peasant

guante (GWAHN-tay) n. glove

guapo (GWAH-poh) adj. handsome

güero (GWAY-roh) n. *Mex.* blond; fair complexion

guía (GHEE-ah) n. guide

guía telefónica (GHEE-ah tay-lay-FOH-nee-cah)
    n. *Cuba, Ec., Pe., RP, Ven.* telephone directory

guineo (ghee-NAY-oh) n. *Pan., PR* small banana

guisado (ghee-SAH-doh) n. stew

guiso (GHEE-soh) n. dish; *PR* stew

guitarra (ghee-TAH-rah) n. guitar

gustar (goo-STAHR) v. like

H

haber (ah-BAYR) v. have (auxiliary)

habichuelas (ah-bee-CHWAY-lahs) n. *Mex., Pan.*
    green beans

habitación (ah-bee-tah-see-OHN) n. room

hablar (ah-BLAHR) v. speak

hace (AH-say) adv. ago (ex. **hace un año**, a
    year ago)

hacer (ah-SAYR) v. do; make

hacia (AH-see-ah) prep. toward

hambre (AHM-bray) n. hunger

hamburguesa (ahm-boor-GAY-sah) n. hamburger

hasta (AH-stah) prep. until

hay (AH-ee) v. there is; there are

helado (ay-LAH-doh) n. ice cream

hermana (ayr-MAH-nah) n. sister

hermano (ayr-MAH-noh) n. brother

hermoso (ayr-MOH-soh) adj. beautiful

hielo (ee-AY-loh) n. ice

hija (EE-hah) n. daughter

hijo (EE-hoh) n. son

hoja (OH-hah) n. leaf; sheet (of paper)

hoja de afeitar (OH-hah day ah-fay-TAHR) n. razor blade

hoja de rasurar (OH-hah day rah-soo-RAHR) n. *Mex.* razor blade

hombre (OHM-bray) n. man

hombre de negocios (OHM-bray day nay-GOH-see-ohs) n. businessman

honesto (oh-NAYS-toh) adj. honest

hora (OH-rah) n. hour; time

horario (oh-RAH-ree-oh) n. schedule

horrible (oh-REE-blay) adj. horrible

hospital (ohs-pee-TAHL) n. hospital

hotel (oh-TAYL) n. hotel

hoy (oy) n., adv. today

hueco (WAY-coh) n. hole

huésped (WAYS-payd) n. guest

huevo (WAY-voh) n. egg

I

idea (ee-DAY-ah) n. idea

idioma (ee-dee-OH-mah) n. language

iglesia (ee-GLAY-see-ah) n. church

ilegal (ee-lay-GAHL) adj. illegal

imagen (ee-MAH-hen) n. image

imaginar (ee-mah-hee-NAHR) v. imagine

imperdible (eem-payr-DEE-blay) n. *Ec.* bobby pin

impermeable (eem-payr-may-AH-blay) n. raincoat

importaciones (eem-pohr-tah-see-OH-nays) n. imports

importador (eem-pohr-tah-DOHR) n. importer

importancia (eem-pohr-TAHN-see-ah) n. importance

importante (eem-pohr-TAHN-tay) adj. important

importar (eem-pohr-TAHR) v. import; matter

imposible (eem-poh-SEE-blay) adj. impossible

impresión (eem-pray-see-OHN) n. impression; printing

impresionante (eem-pray-see-oh-NAHN-tay) adj. impressive

impresionar (eem-pray-see-oh-NAHR) v. make an impression

impresor (eem-pray-SOHR) n. printer

impuesto (eem-PWAYS-toh) n. tax

impuesto de utilidades (eem-PWAYS-toh day oo-tee-lee-DAH-days) n. income tax

incluir (een-cloo-EER) v. include

incluso (een-CLOO-soh) adv. even

independiente (een-day-payn-dee-AYN-tay) adj. independent

indicar (een-dee-CAHR) v. indicate

industria (een-DOO-stree-ah) n. industry

inferior (een-fay-ree-OHR) adj. inferior; lower

informar (een-fohr-MAHR) v. inform

informe (een-FOHR-may) n. report

ingresos (een-GRAY-sohs) n. income

inmediatamente (een-may-dee-ah-tah-MAYN-tay) adv. immediately

inmigrante (een-mee-GRAHN-tay) n. immigrant

inodoro (een-oh-DOH-roh) n. toilet

insecto (een-SAYK-toh) n. insect

insistir (een-see-STEER) v. insist

inspeccionar (een-spayk-see-oh-NAHR) v. inspect

instituto (een-stee-TOO-toh) n. institute

instrucción (een-strook-see-OHN) n. instruction

insultar (een-sool-TAHR) v. insult

inteligente (een-tay-lee-HAYN-tay) adj. intelligent

intentar (een-tayn-TAHR) v. try; attempt

intérprete (een-TAYR-pray-tay) n. interpreter

invierno (een-vee-AYR-noh) n. winter; *SA* rainy season

invitación (een-vee-tah-see-OHN) n. invitation

invitado (een-vee-TAH-doh) n. guest

invitar (een-vee-TAHR) v. invite

ir (eer) v. go

ir de compras (eer day COHM-prahs) v. go shopping

ir de prisa (eer day PREE-sah) v. hurry

ir(se) (EER-say) v. go away

isla (EES-lah) n. island

izquierdo (ees-key-AYR-doh) adj. left

J

jabón (hah-BOHN) n. soap

jalar (hah-LAHR) v. pull

jamón (hah-MOHN) n. ham

jardín (hahr-DEEN) n. garden

jefe (HAY-fay) n. chief; boss

jíbaro (HEE-bah-roh) n. *PR* peasant

jitomate (hee-toh-MAH-tay) n. *Mex.* tomato

joven (HOH-vayn) n. young person; adj. young

joyería (hoh-yay-REE-ah) n. jewelry store

jueves (HWAY-vays) n. Thursday

jugar (hoo-GAHR) v. play; gamble

jugo de naranja (HOO-goh day nah-RAHN-hah)
　　n. orange juice

julio (HOO-lee-oh) n. July

junio (HOON-nee-oh) n. June

justicia (hoos-TEE-see-ah) n. justice

K

kilo(gramo) (key-loh-GRAH-moh) n. kilogram

kilómetro (key-LOH-may-troh) n. kilometer
　　(approx. 5/8 mile)

L

la (lah) fem. art. the

ladrón (lah-DROHN) n. thief

lago (LAH-goh) n. lake

lámpara (LAHM-pah-rah) n. lamp

lana (LAH-nah) n. wool; *Mex.* money (slang)

langosta (lahn-GOH-stah) n. lobster

lápiz (LAH-pees) n. pencil

largo (LAHR-goh) adj. long

las (lahs) f. plu. art. the

las onces (lahs OHN-says) n. *Chi.* snack

lata (LAH-tah) n. can

lavandería (lah-vahn-day-REE-ah) n. laundry

lavar (lah-VAHR) v. wash

leche (LAY-chay) n. milk

lechuga (lay-CHOO-gah) n. lettuce

leer (lay-AYR) v. read

lejos (LAY-hohs) adv. far

lente (LAYN-tay) n. lens

lentes (LAYN-tays) n. *Mex.* eyeglasses

levantar (lay-vahn-TAHR) v. raise; lift

ley (lay) n. law

libertad (lee-bayr-TAHD) n. freedom

libra (LEE-brah) n. pound

libre (LEE-bray) adj. free

libro (LEE-broh) n. book

licencia (lee-SAYN-see-ah) n. license

licenciado (lee-sayn-see-AH-doh) n. *Mex.* lawyer

licor (lee-COHR) n. liquor; liqueur

limón (lee-MOHN) n. lemon; lime

limonada (lee-moh-NAH-dah) n. lemonade

limosnero (lee-mohs-NAY-roh) n. beggar

limpiabotas (leem-pee-ah-BOH-tahs) n. *Carib.*,
   Ven. shoeshine boy

limpio (LEEM-pee-oh) adj. clean

lindo (LEEN-doh) adj. pretty

lista (LEE-stah) n. list

listo (LEE-stoh) adj. ready; clever

llamar (yah-MAHR) v. call

llamar por teléfono (yah-MAHR pohr tay-LAY-foh-noh) v. phone

llanta (YAHN-tah) n. *Mex., Uru.* tire

llave (YAH-vay) n. key; *Mex., Pe.* faucet

llegada (yay-GAH-dah) n. arrival

llegar (yay-GAHR) v. arrive

lleno (YAY-noh) adj. full

llevar (yay-VAHR) v. take

llover (yoh-VAYR) v. rain

lluvia (YOO-vee-ah) n. rain

loco (LOH-coh) adj. crazy

los (lohs) m. plu. art. the

lotería (loh-tay-REE-ah) n. lottery

lucha (LOO-chah) n. struggle

lugar (loo-GAHR) n. place

lujo (LOO-hoh) n. luxury

luna de miel (LOO-nah dạy mee-AYL) n. honeymoon

luz (loos) n. light

M

madera (mah-DAY-rah) n. wood

madre (MAH-dray) n. mother; *Mex.* (has vulgar meaning)

mal (mahl) n. evil; adj. bad

malo (MAH-loh) adj. bad; sick

manejar (mah-nay-HAHR) v. manage; drive

mango (MAHN-goh) n. mango

maní (mah-NEE) n. peanuts (except in *Mex.*)

manija (mah-NEE-hah) n. handle

mano (MAH-noh) n. hand

manteca (mahn-TAY-cah) n. lard; *RP* butter

mantecado (mahn-tay-CAH-doh) n. *PR* ice cream

mantener (mahn-tay-NAYR) v. maintain; keep

mantequilla (mahn-tay-KEY-yah) n. butter (except *RP*)

manzana (mahn-SAH-nah) n. apple

mañana (mah-NYAH-nah) n. morning; adv. tomorrow

mapa (MAH-pah) n. map

máquina (MAH-key-nah) n. machine; *Cuba* taxi

máquina de afeitar (MAH-key-nah day ah-fay-TAHR) n. razor

mar (mahr) n. sea

marca (MAHR-cah) n. brand

marisco (mah-REES-coh) n. shellfish

martes (MAHR-tays) n. Tuesday

marzo (MAHR-soh) n. March

más (mahs) adv. more; most

matar (mah-TAHR) v. kill

mayo (MAH-yoh) n. May

me (may) pron. me; to me

mecánico (may-CAH-nee-coh) n. mechanic; adj. mechanical

medias (MAY-dee-ahs) n. socks

medicina (may-dee-SEE-nah) n. medicine

médico (MAY-dee-coh) n. doctor; adj. medical

medio (MAY-dee-oh) n., adj. half; middle

mediodía (may-dee-oh-DEE-ah) n. noon

medusa (may-DOO-sah) n. *Bol., Uru.* jelly fish

mientras (que) (mee-AYN-trahs kay) conj. while

mejor (may-HOHR) adj. better; best

mejorar (may-hoh-RAHR) v. improve

melocotón (may-loh-coh-TOHN) n. *Carib., Pe.* peach

melón (may-LOHN) n. melon; *Cuba* watermelon

mendigo (mayn-DEE-goh) n. beggar

menor (may-NOHR) adj. less; least; smaller; younger

menos (MAY-nohs) adj., adv. less

mentira (mayn-TEE-rah) n. lie

mercado (mayr-CAH-doh) n. market

merienda (mayr-ree-AYN-dah) n. snack

mercancía (mayr-cahn-SEE-ah) n. merchandise; goods

mermelada (mayr-may-LAH-dah) n. jam

mes (mays) n. month

mesa (MAY-sah) n. table

mesera (may-SAY-rah) n. *Mex.* waitress

mesero (may-SAY-roh) n. *Mex.* waiter

metro (MAY-troh) n. meter (measurement); *Mex.* subway

mi (mee) adj. my

miedo (mee-AY-doh) n. fear

miércoles (mee-AYR-coh-lays) n. Wednesday

mil (meel) n., adj. thousand

milla (MEE-yah) n. mile

millón (mee-YOHN) n. million

minuto (mee-NOO-toh) n. minute

mirar (mee-RAHR) v. look at

mismo (MEES-moh) adj., pron. same

molestar (moh-lays-TAHR) v. bother

momento (moh-MAYN-toh) n. moment

moneda (moh-NAY-dah) n. coin

montaña (mohn-TAH-nyah) n. mountain

morado (moh-RAH-doh) adj. purple

moreno (moh-RAY-noh) adj. dark

morir (moh-REER) v. die

mosca (MOHS-cah) n. fly

mosquito (mohs-KEY-toh) n. mosquito

mostrar (mohs-TRAHR) v. show

motocicleta (moh-toh-see-CLAY-tah) n. motorcycle

motor (moh-TOHR) n. motor; engine

mozo (MOH-soh) n. *Ec., Pe., RP* waiter

muchacha (moo-CHAH-chah) n. girl

muchacho (moo-CHAH-choh) n. boy

mucho (MOO-choh) adj., adv. much

muchos (MOO-chohs) adj., pron. many

muebles (moo-AY-blays) n. furniture

muela (moo-AY-lah) n. molar

muestra (moo-AYS-trah) n. sample

mujer (moo-HAYR) n. woman

mundo (MOON-doh) n. world

museo (moo-SAY-oh) n. museum

música (MOO-see-cah) n. music

muy (MOO-ee) adv. very

¡Muy bien! (MOO-ee bee-AYN) interj. Very well!; Fine!

N

nacimiento (nah-see-mee-AYN-toh) n. birth

nación (nah-see-OHN) n. nation

nacional (nah-see-oh-NAHL) adj. national

nada (NAH-dah) pron. nothing

nadar (nah-DAHR) v. swim

nadie (NAH-dee-ay) pron. nobody; no one

nafta (NAHF-tah) n. *Arg.* gas

naranja (nah-RAHN-hah) n. orange

nariz (nah-REES) n. nose

Navidad (nah-vee-DAHD) n. Christmas

necesario (nay-say-SAH-ree-oh) adj. necessary

necesitar (nay-say-see-TAHR) v. need

negocio (nay-GOH-see-oh) n. business

negro (NAY-groh) n., adj. black

neumático (nay-oo-MAH-tee-coh) n. *Chi., Uru.* tire

ni (nee) conj. neither

nieto (nee-AY-toh) n. grandson

ninguno (neen-GOO-noh) adj. no; not any; pron. none

niña (NEE-nyah) n. girl

niño (NEE-nyoh) n. boy

no (noh) adv. no; not

noche (NOH-chay) n. night

nombre (NOHM-bray) n. name

norte (NOHR-tay) n. north

nosotros (noh-SOH-trohs) pron. we

nota (NOH-tah) n. note

notar (noh-TAHR) v. note

noticias (noh-TEE-see-ahs) n. news

noventa (noh-VAYN-tah) n., adj. ninety

novia (NOH-vee-ah) n. girlfriend; bride

noviembre (noh-vee-AYM-bray) n. November

novio (NOH-vee-oh) n. boyfriend; groom

nuestro (noo-AYS-troh) adj. our

nueve (noo-AY-vay) n., adj. nine

nuevo (noo-AY-voh) adj. new

número (NOO-may-roh) n. number

nunca (NOON-cah) adv. never

O

o (oh) conj. or; either

objetos de valor (ohb-HAY-tohs day vah-LOHR) n. valuables

observar (ohb-sayr-VAHR) v. observe

obtener (ohb-tay-NAYR) v. obtain; get

ochenta (oh-CHAYN-tah) n., adj. eighty

ocho (OH-choh) n., adj. eight

octubre (ok-TOO-bray) n. October

ocupación (oh-coo-pah-see-OHN) n. occupation

ocupar (oh-cooh-PAHR) v. occupy

ocurrir (oh-coo-REER) v. occur; happen

odiar (oh-dee-AHR) v. hate

oeste (oh-AY-stay) n. west

oficial (oh-fee-see-AHL) n. official; officer; adj. official

oficina (oh-fee-SEE-nah) n. office

oficina de correos (oh-fee-SEE-nah day coh-RAY-ohs) n. *Mex.* post office

ofrecer (oh-fray-SAYR) v. offer

ofrecimiento (oh-fray-see-mee-AYN-toh) n. offer

oír (oh-EER) v. hear

ojo (OH-hoh) n. eye

olvidar (ohl-vee-DAHR) v. forget

omitir (oh-mee-TEER) v. omit

once (OHN-say) n., adj. eleven

onza (OHN-sah) n. ounce

oportunidad (oh-pohr-too-nee-DAHD) n. opportunity

orden (OHR-dayn) n. order

orden de pago (OHR-dayn day PAH-goh) n. money order

organización (ohr-gah-nee-sah-see-OHN) n. organization

oro (OH-roh) n. gold

oscuro (ohs-COO-roh) adj. dark

otoño (oh-TOH-nyoh) n. autumn; fall

otra vez (OH-trah vays) adv. again

otro (OH-troh) adj. other; another

P

padre (PAH-dray) n. father; adj. *Mex., Pe.* terrific (slang)

padres (PAH-drays) n. parents

pagar (pah-GAHR) v. pay; pay for

página (PAH-hee-nah) n. page

pago (PAH-goh) n. payment

país (pah-EES) n. country; nation

paisaje (pah-ee-SAH-hay) n. landscape

pájaro (PAH-hah-roh) n. bird

pajita (pah-HEE-tah) n. *Chi., Uru.* drinking straw

palabra (pah-LAH-brah) n. word

palomitas (pah-loh-MEE-tahs) n. *Mex.* popcorn

pan (pahn) n. bread

panadería (pah-nah-day-REE-ah) n. bakery

pantalones (pahn-tah-LOHN-nays) n. trousers; pants

papa (PAH-pah) n. potato

papel (pah-PAYL) n. paper

papelería (pah-pay-lay-REE-ah) n. stationery store

paquete (pah-KAY-tay) n. package

para (PAH-rah) prep. to; for

parada (pah-RAH-dah) n. bus stop

paradero (pah-rah-DAY-roh) n. *Chi., Col.* bus stop

paraguas (pah-RAH-gwahs) n. umbrella

pardo (PAHR-doh) adj. brown

parecer (pah-ray-SAYR) v. seem; appear

pared (pah-RAYD) n. wall

pareja (pah-RAY-hah) n. couple

parque (PAHR-kay) n. park

parquear (pahr-kay-AHR) v. *Bol., Cuba* park

parqueo (pahr-KAY-oh) n. *Bol., Cuba* parking lot

parte (PAHR-tay) n. part

participar (pahr-tee-see-PAHR) v. participate

pasado (pah-SAH-doh) n., adj. past

pasador (pah-sah-DOHR) n. *Mex., Uru.* bobby pin

pasajero (pah-sah-HAY-roh) n. passenger

pasamano (pah-sah-MAH-noh) n. handrail

pasaporte (pah-sah-POHR-tay) n. passport

pasar (pah-SAHR) v. pass; *Arg., Ven.* pass (in car)

pasillo (pah-SEE-yoh) n. hall

pastel (pah-STAYL) n. pie; *Mex.* cake

pastelería (pah-stay-lay-REE-ah) n. bakery

patria (PAH-tree-ah) n. homeland

pay (PAH-ee) n. *Mex.* pie

peatón (pay-ah-TOHN) n. pedestrian

pedir (pay-DEER) v. ask for; order

pegamento (pay-gah-MAYN-toh) n. *Mex., Uru.* glue

película (pay-LEE-coo-lah) n. film

peligro (pay-LEE-groh) n. danger

peligroso (pay-lee-GROH-soh) adj. dangerous

pelo (PAY-loh) n. hair

peluquería (pay-loo-kay-REE-ah) n. beauty shop; barbershop (except *Cuba*)

peluquero (pay-loo-KAY-roh) n. hairdresser; barber (except *Cuba*)

pendientes (payn-dee-AYN-tays) n. *Cuba* dangling earrings

pensar (payn-SAHR) n. think

peor (pay-OHR) adj. adv. worse; worst

pepino (pay-PEE-noh) n. cucumber

pequeño (pay-KAY-nyoh) adj. small; *Ven.* short (person)

perchero (payr-CHAY-roh) n. *Cuba* clothes hanger

perder (payr-DAYR) v. lose

perdón (payr-DOHN) n. pardon

perfume (payr-FOO-may) n. perfume

periódico (pay-ree-OH-dee-coh) n. newspaper

perla (PAYR-lah) n. pearl

permiso (payr-MEE-soh) n. permission; permit

permiso de manejo (payr-MEE-soh day mah-NAY-hoh) n. *Arg.* driver's license

permitir (payr-mee-TEER) v. permit

pero (PAY-roh) conj. but

perro (PAY-roh) n. dog

perro caliente (PAY-roh cah-lee-AYN-tay) n. *Cuba, Mex.* hot dog

persona (payr-SOH-nah) n. person

personal (payr-soh-NAHL) n. personnel; adj. personal

pertenecer (payr-tay-nay-SAYR) v. belong

pesca (PAYS-cah) n. fishing

pescado (pays-CAH-doh) n. fish (as food)

pesero (pay-SAY-roh) n. *Mex.* jitney

peso (PAY-soh) n. weight; peso (currency)

petróleo (pay-TROH-lay-oh) n. petroleum; gas

picante (pee-CAHN-tay) adj. hot (spicy)

pico (PEE-coh) n. beak; peak

pie (pee-AY) n. foot

piel (pee-AYL) n. skin

pierna (pee-AYR-nah) n. leg

pieza (pee-AY-sah) n. piece; *Arg., Chi.* room

pijamas (pee-CHAH-mahs) n. pajamas

pila (PEE-lah) n. battery

pimienta (pee-mee-AYN-tah) n. black pepper

pintor (peen-TOHR) n. painter

piña (PEE-nyah) n. pineapple (except *Arg.*)

pipocas (pee-POH-cahs) n. *Bol.* popcorn

pirámide (pee-RAH-mee-day) n. pyramid

piscina (pee-SEE-nah) n. swimming pool (except *Arg.* and *Mex.*)

piso (PEE-soh) n. floor

plancha (PLAHN-chah) n. iron

planta (PLAHN-tah) n. plant

planta baja (PLAHN-tah BAH-hah) n. *Mex.* ground floor

plantar (plahn-TAHR) v. plant

plata (PLAH-tah) n. silver; money (slang)

plátano (PLAH-tah-noh) n. banana

plato (PLAH-toh) n. plate; dish

playa (PLAH-yah) n. beach

plaza mayor (PLAH-sah mah-YOHR) n. main square

pluma (PLOO-mah) n. pen

pobre (POH-bray) adj. poor

poco (POH-coh) adj., pron. little

pocos (POH-cohs) adj., pron. few

poder (poh-DAYR) n. power; v. be able to

policía (poh-lee-SEE-ah) n. police

policía acostado (poh-lee-SEE-ah ah-cohs-TAH-doh) n. *Ec.* speed bumps

política (poh-LEE-tee-cah) n. policy; politics

pollo (POH-yoh) n. chicken

pomelo (poh-MAY-loh) n. *Arg.* grapefruit

poner (poh-NAYR) v. put; place

poner(se) (poh-NAYR-say) v. put on

popotes (poh-POH-tays) n. *Mex.* drinking straws

por (pohr) prep. by; through; by way of

porcentaje (pohr-sayn-TAH-hay) n. percentage

por ciento (pohr see-AYN-toh) adv. percent

porotos (poh-ROH-tohs) n. *Chi.* dry beans

porotos verdes (poh-ROH-tohs VAYR-days) n. *Chi.* green beans

porque (POHR-kay) conj. because

¿por qué? (pohr kay) interr. why?

posible (poh-SEE-blay) adj. possible

posición (poh-see-see-OHN) n. position

postre (POH-stray) n. dessert

practicar (prahk-tee-CAHR) v. practice

precio (PRAY-see-oh) n. price

preciso (pray-SEE-soh) adj. necessary

preferir (pray-fay-REER) v. prefer

pregunta (pray-GOON-tah) n. question

preguntar (pray-goon-TAHR) v. ask (question)

preocupar(se) (pray-oh-coo-PAHR-say) v. be worried

preparar (pray-pah-RAHR) v. prepare

presentación (pray-sayn-tah-see-OHN) n. presentation; appearance

presentar (pray-sayn-TAHR) v. present

presidente (pray-see-DAYN-tay) n. president

prestar (pray-STAHR) v. lend

presupuesto (pray-soo-PWAY-stoh) n. budget

primavera (pree-mah-VAY-rah) n. spring

primero (pree-MAY-roh) adj. first

principal (preen-see-PAHL) adj. principal; main

prisión (pree-see-OHN) n. prison

privado (pree-VAH-doh) adj. private

probable (proh-BAH-blay) adj. probable

probar (proh-BAHR) v. prove; try

probar(se) (proh-BAHR-say) v. try on

problema (proh-BLAY-mah) n. problem

producir (proh-doo-SEER) v. produce

producto (proh-DOOK-toh) n. product

profundo (proh-FOON-doh) adj. deep

prohibir (proh-ee-BEER) v. prohibit

promedio (proh-MAY-dee-oh) n. average

prometer (proh-may-TAYR) v. promise

pronto ((PROHN-toh) adv. quick; *Uru.* right now

propina (proh-PEE-nah) n. tip

propósito (proh-POH-see-toh) n. purpose

prostituta (proh-stee-TOO-tah) n. prostitute

protección (proh-tayk-see-OHN) n. protection

próximo (PROKH-see-moh) adj. next

público (POO-blee-coh) n. public; audience; adj. public

pueblo (PWAY-bloh) n. people; town

puente (PWAYN-tay) n. bridge

puerta (PWAYR-tah) n. door

puerto (PWAYR-toh) n. port

pulgada (pool-GAH-dah) n. inch

pulsera (pool-SAY-rah) n. bracelet

puntual (poon-too-AHL) adj. punctual

puro (POO-roh) n. *Mex. Pe.* cigar; adj. pure

Q

que (kay) pron. that; which; who; whom

¿qué? (kay) adj., pron. What? Which?

quedar(se) (kay-DAHR-say) v. remain

quejar (kay-HAHR) v. complain

quemar (kay-MAHR) v. burn

querer (kay-RAYR) v. wish; want; love

queso (KAY-soh) n. cheese

¿quién? (key-AYN) interr. Who? Whom?

quince (KEYN-say) n., adj. fifteen

quitar (key-TAHR) v. take away

quitar(se) (key-TAHR-say) v. take off

quizás (key-SAHS) adv. perhaps

R

radio (RAH-dee-oh) n. radio

rápido (RAH-pee-doh) adj. fast

rasurar (rah-soo-RAHR) v. *Mex.* shave

rayos X (RAH-yohs AYK-ees) n. X-rays

realmente (ray-ahl-MAYN-tay) adv. really

recado (ray-CAH-doh) n. message

recámara (ray-CAH-mah-rah) n. *Mex.* bedroom

receta (ray-SAY-tah) n. prescription; recipe

recibir (ray-see-VEER) v. receive

recibo (ray-SEE-boh) n. receipt

reciente (ray-see-AYN-tay) adj. recent

reclamar (ray-clah-MAHR) v. claim

recoger (ray-coh-HAYR) v. pick up

recomendar (ray-coh-mayn-DAHR) n. recommend

reconocer (ray-coh-noh-SAYR) v. recognize

reconocimiento (ray-coh-noh-see-mee-AYN-toh) n. recognition

recordar (ray-cohr-DAHR) v. remember

recuerdo (ray-KWAYR-doh) n. memory; souvenir

referir (ray-fay-REER) v. refer

refresco (ray-FRAYS-coh) n. soft drink

regalo (ray-GAH-loh) n. gift

regatear (ray-gah-tay-AHR) v. bargain

regateo (ray-gah-TAY-oh) n. bargaining

registro (ray-HEE-stroh) n. registration

regresar (ray-gray-SAHR) v. return

rehusar (ray-oo-SAHR) v. refuse

reloj (ray-LOH) n. clock; watch

remitir (ray-mee-TEER) v. forward

remolacha (ray-moh-LAH-chah) n. beet (except *Mex.*)

repetir (ray-pay-TEER) v. repeat

reservación (ray-sayr-vah-see-OHN) n.
reservation

reservar (ray-sayr-VAHR) v. reserve

resfriado (rays-free-AH-doh) n. head cold

resolver (ray-sohl-VAYR) v. resolve

responder (rays-pohn-DAYR) v. respond

responsable (rays-pohn-SAH-blay) adj.
responsible

respuesta (rays-PWAY-stah) n. reply

restaurante (rays-tah-oo-RAHN-tay) n. restaurant

retraso (ray-TRAH-soh) n. delay

reunión (ray-oo-nee-OHN) n. meeting

revelar (ray-vay-LAHR) v. develop (film)

revista (ray-VEE-stah) n. magazine

rico (REE-coh) adj. rich; delicious

río (REE-oh) n. river

risa (REE-sah) n. laughter

robar (roh-BAHR) v. rob; steal

rodilla (roh-DEE-yah) n. knee

rojo (ROH-hoh) n., adj. red

romper (rohm-PAYR) v. break

ron (rohn) n. rum

ropa (ROH-pah) n. clothes

ropa interior (ROH-pah een-tay-ree-OHR) n.
underwear

rosado (roh-SAH-doh) n., adj. pink

rositas de maíz (roh-SAY-tahs day mah-EES) n.
Cuba popcorn

roto (ROH-toh) adj. broken

rubí (roo-BEE) n. ruby

rubio (ROO-bee-oh) n., adj. blond; fair
complected (person)

rueda (roo-AY-dah) n. wheel

ruido (roo-EE-doh) n. noise

ruta (ROO-tah) n. route

S

sábado (SAH-bah-doh) n. Saturday

sábana (SAH-bah-nah) n. sheet

saber (sah-BAYR) v. know; know how to

sabroso (sah-BROH-soh) adj. delicious

sacar foto (sah-CAHR FOH-toh) v. take a picture

sal (sahl) n. salt

sala (SAH-lah) n. *Cuba, Mex., Uru.* living room

salario (sah-LAH-ree-oh) n. wages

salchicha (sahl-CHEE-chah) n. sausage; *Mex.* frankfurter

salida (sah-LEE-dah) n. exit; departure

salir (sah-LEER) v. come out; leave

salón de belleza (sah-LOHN day bay-YAY-sah) n. beauty shop

salsa (SAHL-sah) n. sauce; *Carib.* tropical dance music

salsa picante (SAHL-sah pee-CAHN-tay) n. chilli sauce

saltar (sahl-TAHR) v. jump

salud (sah-LOOD) n. health

saludar (sah-loo-DAHR) v. greet

saludo (sah-LOO-doh) n. greeting

salvar (sahl-VAHR) v. save

sánduche (SAHN-doo-chay) n. *Ec.* sandwich

sandwich (SAHND-oo-eech) n. sandwich

sano (SAH-noh) adj. healthy

satisfactorio (sah-tees-fahk-TOH-ree-oh) adj. satisfactory

saya (SAH-yah) n. *Cuba* skirt

seco (SAY-coh) adj. dry

secretario (say-cray-TAH-ree-oh) n. secretary

seda (SAY-dah) n. silk

seguir (say-GHEER) v. follow; continue

según (say-GOON) prep. according to

seguramente (say-goo-ree-MAYN-tay) adv. surely

seguridad (say-goo-ree-DAHD) n. security

seguro (say-GOO-roh) adj. sure; safe

seguro de vida (say-GOO-roh day VEE-dah) n. life insurance

seis (says) n., adj. six

selva (SAYL-vah) n. jungle; woods

sello (SAY-yoh) n. stamp; seal

semana (say-MAH-nah) n. week

sencillo (sayn-SEE-yoh) adj. simple; single

sentar (sayn-TAHR) v. seat

sentar(se) sayn-TAHR-say) v. sit down

sentir(se) (sayn-TEER-say) v. feel; be sorry

señor (say-NYOHR) n. sir; Mr.

señora (say-NYOH-rah) n. Mrs.

señorita (say-nyoh-REE-tah) n. Miss; young lady

separación (say-pah-rah-see-OHN) n. separation

separado (say-pah-RAH-doh) adj. separate

separar (say-pah-RAHR) v. separate

septiembre (sayp-tee-AYM-bray) n. September

ser (sayr) n. being; essence; v. be

servicio (sayr-VEE-see-oh) n. service; restroom

servilleta (sayr-vee-YAY-tah) n. napkin

servir (sayr-VEER) v. serve

sesenta (say-SAYN-tah) n., adj. sixty

setenta (say-TAYN-tah) n., adj. seventy

si (see) conj. if; whether

sí (see) adv. yes; indeed

siempre (see-AYM-pray) adv. always

siesta (see-AY-stah) n. midday rest

siete (see-AY-tay) n., adj. seven

silla (SEE-yah) n. chair

simpático (seem-PAH-tee-coh) adj. nice; charming

sin (seen) prep. without

sindicato (seen-dee-CAH-toh) n. labor union

sin embargo (seen aym-BAHR-goh) adv. nevertheless

sirvienta (seer-vee-AYN-tah) n. maid

sirviente (seer-vee-AYN-tay) n. servant

sistema (sees-TAY-mah) n. system

sobre (SOH-bray) prep. on; upon

sobrepeso (soh-bray-PAY-soh) n. overweight

sociedad (soh-see-ay-DAHD) n. society; company

socio (SOH-see-oh) n. partner; *Cuba* buddy

¡Socorro! (soh-COH-roh) imper. Help!

sol (sohl) n. sun

solamente (soh-lah-MAYN-tay) adv. only

solo (SOH-loh) adj. only; alone

soltero(a) (sohl-TAY-roh/rah) n., adj. single

sombrero (sohm-BRAY-roh) n. hat

sopa (SOH-pah) n. soup

sótano (SOH-tah-noh) n. basement

su (soo) adj. his; her; its; their; your; one's

subir (soo-VEER) v. go up

subterráneo (soob-tay-RAH-nay-oh) n. *Arg., Bol.* subway

suciedad (soo-see-ay-DAHD) n. dirt

sucio (SOO-see-oh) adj. dirty

sucursal (soo-coor-SAHL) n. (com.) branch

sudamericano (sood-ah-may-ree-CAH-noh) n., adj. South American

suela (SWAY-lah) n. sole of shoe

sueldo (SWAYL-doh) n. salary

sueño (SWAY-nyo) n. dream; sleep

suerte (SWAYR-tay) n. luck

suéter (SWAY-tayr) n. sweater

sumamente (soo-mah-MAYN-tay) adv. extremely

sur (soor) n. south

T

tabaco (tah-BAH-coh) n. tobacco; *CA, Cuba, Ven.* cigar

tacón (tah-COHN) n. heel

tacho (TAH-choh) n. *Arg.* taxi

tal (tahl) adj. such; such a

tal vez (tahl vays) adv. perhaps

tamaño (tah-MAH-nyoh) n. size

también (tahm-bee-AYN) adv. too; also

tan pronto como (tahn-PROHN-toh COH-moh) conj. as soon as

tapa (TAH-pah) n. cover; lid

tapete (tah-PAY-tay) n. *Mex.* throw rug

taquilla (tah-KEY-yah) n. box office; *CR* tavern

tarde (TAHR-day) n. afternoon; adv. late

tarifa (tah-REE-fah) n. tariff; fare

tarjeta (tahr-HAY-tah) n. card

trajeta de presentación (tahr-HAY-tah day pray-sayn-tah-see-OHN) n. business card

tarjeta postal (tahr-HAY-tah pohs-TAHL) n. postcard

taxi (TAHK-see) n. taxi

taza (TAH-sah) n. cup; toilet bowl

tazón (tah-SOHN) n. bowl

té (tay) n. tea

teatro (tay-AH-troh) n. theater

técnico (TAYK-nee-coh) n. technician; adj. technical

tela (TAY-lah) n. cloth

teléfono (tay-LAY-foh-noh) n. telephone

telegrama (tay-lay-GRAH-mah) n. telegram

temblor (taym-BLOHR) n. earthquake

temperatura (taym-pay-rah-too-rah) n. temperature

temprano (taym-PRAH-noh) adj., adv. early

tenedor (tay-nay-DOHR) n. fork

tener (tay-NAYR) v. have; own

tener hambre (tay-NAYR AHM-bray) v. be hungry

tener que (tay-NAYR kay) v. have to; must

tener sed (tay-NAYR sayd) v. be thirsty

tenis (TAY-nees) n. tennis

ternera (tayr-NAY-rah) n. veal

terrible (tay-REE-blay) adj. terrible

tiburón (tee-boo-ROHN) n. shark

tiempo (tee-AYM-poh) n. time; weather

tienda (tee-AYN-dah) n. store; *Pe.* department store

tienda de campaña (tee-AYN-dah day cahm-PAH-nyah) n. tent

tienda de departamentos (tee-AYN-dah day day-pahr-tah-MAYN-tohs) n. department store

tierra (tee-AY-rah) n. land; earth

tijeras (tee-HAY-rahs) n. scissors

timbre (TEEM-bray) n. bell; *Mex.* postage stamp

tina (TEE-nah) n. *Mex.* bathtub

típico (TEE-pee-coh) adj. typical

tipo de cambio (TEE-poh day CAHM-bee-oh) n. rate of exchange

tirar (tee-RAHR) v. pull

toalla (toh-AH-yah) n. towel

tobillo (toh-BEE-yoh) n. ankle

tocar (toh-CAHR) v. touch; knock; play (instrument)

tocino (toh-SEE-noh) n. bacon

todavía (toh-dah-VEE-ah) adv. still; yet

todo (TOH-doh) adj. all; every

todo el mundo (TOH-doh el MOON-doh) pron. everybody

tomate (toh-MAH-tay) n. tomato

tomar (toh-MAHR) v. take; eat; drink

topes (TOH-pays) n. *Mex.* speed bumps

toronja (toh-ROHN-hah) n. grapefruit

torta (TOHR-tah) n. *Arg.* pie; *Ec.* cake; *Mex.* sandwich on roll; *Uru.* pancake

tortilla (tohr-TEE-yah) n. tortilla; *Cuba* omelet

trabajar (trah-bah-HAHR) v. work

trabajo (trah-BAH-hoh) n. work

traducción (trah-dook-see-OHN) n. translation

traducir (trah-doo-SEER) v. translate

traer (trah-AYR) v. bring

tráfico (TRAH-fee-coh) n. traffic

traje (TRAH-hay) n. suit

tranquilo (trahn-KEY-loh) adj. calm; peaceful

trece (TRAY-say) n., adj. thirteen

treinta (TRAYN-tah) n., adj. thirty

tren (trayn) n. train

tres (trays) n., adj. three

trinche (TREEN-chay) n. *Andes, Mex.* fork

triste (TREE-stay) adj. sad

trucha (TROO-chah) n. trout

tu (too) adj. your (familiar)

tú (too) pron. you (familiar)

U

último (OOL-tee-moh) adj. last

un (oon) masc. art. a; an

una (OON-ah) fem. art. a; an

una vez (OON-ah vays) adv. once

universidad (oo-nee-vayr-see-DAHD) n. university

urbano (oor-BAH-noh) adj. urban

urgente (oor-HAYN-tay) adj. urgent

usar (oo-SAHR) v. use

uso (OO-soh) n. use

usted (oo-STAY) pron. sing. you

ustedes (oo-STAY-days) pron. plu. you

usual (oo-soo-AHL) adj. usual

útil (OO-teel) adj. useful

uva (OO-vah) n. grape

vacancia (vah-CAHN-see-ah) n. vacancy

vacío (vah-SEE-oh) adj. empty

vago (VAH-goh) adj. *Cuba* lazy

vainilla (vah-ee-NEE-yah) n. vanilla

valer (vah-LAYR) v. be worth

válido (VAH-lee-doh) adj. valid

valioso (vah-lee-OH-soh) adj. valuable

valor (vah-LOHR) n. value; courage

valores (vah-LOH-rays) n. valuables

varios (VAH-ree-ohs) adj. various

vaso (VAH-soh) n. drinking glass

vegetal (vay-hay-TAHL) n., adj. vegetable

veinte (VAYN-tay) n., adj. twenty

vela (VAY-lah) n. candle

velocidad (vay-loh-see-DAHD) n. speed

vencido (vayn-SEE-doh) adj. expired

vendedor (vayn-day-DOHR) n. salesman

vender (vayn-DAYR) v. sell

venir (vay-NEER) v. come

venta (VAYN-tay) n. sale; *SD* grocery store

venta al mayoreo (VAYN-tah ahl mah-yoh-RAY-oh) n. wholesale

venta al menudeo (VAYN-tah ahl may-noo-DAY-oh) n. retail

ventaja (vayn-TAH-hah) n. advantage

ventana (vay-TAH-nah) n. window

ver (vayr) v. see

verano (vay-RAH-noh) n. summer

verdadero (vayr-dah-DAY-roh) adj. true; real

verde (VAYR-day) n., adj. green

vestido (vay-STEE-doh) n. dress

viajar (vee-ah-HAHR) v. travel

viaje (vee-AH-hay) n. trip

vida (VEE-dah) n. life

viejo (vee-AY-hoh) n. old man; adj. old

viento (vee-AYN-toh) n. wind

viernes (vee-AYR-nays) n. Friday

vino (VEE-noh) n. wine

vino de Jerez (VEE-noh day hay-RAYS) n. sherry

visa (VEE-sah) n. visa

visitante (vee-see-TAHN-tay) n. visitor

visitar (vee-see-TAHR) v. visit

vista (VEE-stah) n. view

víveres (VEE-vay-rays) n. groceries

vivir (vee-VEER) v. live

volar (voh-LAHR) v. fly

volver (vohl-VAYR) v. return

vomitar (voh-mee-TAHR) v. vomit

vos (vohs) pron. *SA*, used instead of fam. *tú* you

vuelo (VWAY-loh) n. flight

W

whisky (same as in English)

X

xilófono (see-LOH-foh-noh) n. xylophone

Y

y (ee) conj. and
ya (yah) adv. already; now
yate (YAH-tay) n. yacht
yo (yoh) pron. I

Z

zapato (sah-PAH-toh) n. shoe
zócalo (SOH-cah-loh) n. *Mex.* main square
zona (SOH-nah) n. zone
zipper (SEE-payr) n. zipper
zoológico (soh-LOH-hee-coh) n. zoo

ENGLISH-SPANISH DICTIONARY

A

a art. un; una (oon; OO-nah)

aboard adv. a bordo (ah BOHR-doh)

abroad adv. en el extranjero (ayn el ex-trahn-HAY-roh)

absolutely adv. absolutamente (ahb-soh-loo-tah-MAYN-tay)

accelerate v. acelerar (ah-say-lay-RAHR)

accent n. acento (ah-SAYN-toh)

accept v. aceptar (ah-sayp-TAHR)

accident n. accidente (ahk-see-DAYN-tay)

according to prep. según (say-GOON)

account n. cuenta (coo-AYN-tah)

accountant n. contador (cohn-tah-DOHR)

acknowledge v. reconocer (ray-coh-noh-SAYR)

acknowledgement n. reconocimiento (ray-coh-noh-see-mee-AYN-toh)

across prep. a través de (ah trah-VAYS day)

act n. acto (AHK-toh)

action n. acción (ahk-see-OHN)

activity n. actividad (ahk-tee-vee-DAHD)

actor n. actor (ahk-TOHR)

actually adv. realmente (ray-ahl-MAYN-tay)

additional adj. adicional (ah-dee-see-oh-NAHL)

address n. dirección (dee-rayk-see-OHN)

admission n. admisión (ahd-mee-see-OHN)

admit v. admitir (ahd-mee-TEEHR)

advance n. avance v. avanzar (ah-vahn-say; ah-vahn-SAHR)

advantage n. ventaja (vayn-TAH-hah)

advertisement n. anuncio comercial (ah-NOON-see-oh coh-mayr-see-AHL)

advice n. consejo (cohn-SAY-hoh)

after adv. después; prep. después de (days-poo-AYS day)

afternoon n. tarde (TAHR-day)

again adv. otra vez (OH-trah vays)

against prep. contra (COHN-trah)

age n. edad (ay-DAHD)

agency n. agencia (ah-HAYN-see-ah)

agent n. agente (ah-HAYN-tay)

ago adv. hace... (time period) (AH-say...)

agreement n. acuerdo (ah-KUAYR-doh)

air n. aire (AH-ee-ray)

air conditioning n. aire acondicionado; *Mex.* clima (AH-ee-ray ah-cohn-dee-see-oh-NAH-doh; CLEE-mah)

airplane n. avión (ah-vee-OHN)

airport n. aeropuerto (ah-ay-roh-PWAYR-toh)

alarm clock n. despertador (days-payr-tah-DOHR)

alcohol n. alcohol (ahl-COHL)

all adj., pron. todo (TOH-doh)

allow v. permitir (payr-mee-TEEHR)

all right adj., adv. está bien (ays-TAH bee-AYN)

almost adv. casi (CAH-see)

alone adj. solo; adv. solamente (SOH-loh; soh-lah-MAYN-tay)

already adv. ya (yah)

also adv. también (tahm-bee-AYN)

although conj. aunque; sin embargo (ah-OON-kay; seen aym-BAHR-goh)

altitude n. altura (ahl-TOO-rah)

always adv. siempre (see-AYM-pray)

ambassador n. embajador (aym-bah-hah-DOHR)

amber n. ámbar (AHM-bahr)

ambulance n. ambulancia (ahm-boo-LAHN-see-ah)

among prep. entre (AYN-tray)

amount n. cantidad (cahn-tee-DAHD)

amuse v. divertir (dee-vayr-TEER)

an art. un; una (oon; OO-nah)

ancient adj. antiguo (ahn-TEE-gwoh)

and conj. y (ee)

angry adj. enojado (ayn-oh-HAH-doh)

ankle n. tobillo (toh-BEE-yoh)

announce v. anunciar (ah-noon-see-AHR)

annoy v. molestar (moh-lays-TAHR)

annual adj. anual (ah-noo-AHL)

another adj. otro (OH-troh)

answer n. respuesta; v. contestar (rays-PWAY-stah; cohn-tays-TAHR)

antique n. antigüedad (ahn-tee-gway-DAHD)

any pron., adj. alguno (ahl-GOO-noh)

anybody pron. alguien (AHL-ghee-ayn)

anything pron. cualquier cosa (kwal-key-AHR COH-sah)

apart adv. aparte (ah-PAHR-tay)

apartment n. apartamento; *Mex.* departamento (ah-pahr-tah-MAYN-toh; day-pahr-tah-MAYN-toh)

appearance n. presentación (pray-sayn-tah-see-OHN)

apple n. manzana (mahn-SAHN-ah)

appointment n. cita (SEE-tah)

area n. área (AH-ree-ah)

argue v. discutir (dees-coo-TEER)

arm n. brazo (BRAH-soh); (mil.) arma (AHR-mah)

around adv. alrededor (ahl-ray-day-DOHR)

arrange v. arreglar (ah-ray-GLAHR)

arrival n. llegada (yay-GAH-dah)

arrive v. llegar (yay-GAHR)

art n. arte (AHR-tay)

artist n. artista (ahr-TEES-tah)

as conj. como (COH-moh)

ashtray n. cenicero (say-nee-SAY-roh)

ask v. preguntar (pray-goon-TAHR)

ask for v. pedir (pay-DEER)

assets n. capital; (pl.) valores (cah-pee-TAHL; vah-LOH-rays)

assist v. ayudar (ah-yoo-DAHR)

assistant n. asistente (ah-sees-TAYN-tay)

associate n. socio (SOH-see-oh)

as soon as conj. tan pronto como (tahn PROHN-toh COH-moh)

as well as conj. así como (ah-SEE COH-moh)

at prep. a; en (ah;ayn)

at home adv. en casa (ayn CAH-sah)

at least adv. al menos (ahl MAY-nohs)

at once adv. en seguida (ayn say-GHEE-dah)

attempt v. intentar (een-tayn-TAHR)

attend v. asistir (ah-sees-TEER)

at times adv. a veces (ah VAY-says)

attorney n. abogado; *Arg.* boga; *Mex.* licenciado

(ah-boh-GAH-doh; BOH-gah; lee-sayn-see-AH-doh)

aunt n. tía (TEE-ah)

automatic adj. automático (ah-oo-toh-MAH-tee-coh)

autumn n. otoño (oh-TOH-nyoh)

available adj. disponible (dees-pohn-EE-blay)

avenue n. avenida (ah-vay-NEE-dah)

average n. promedio (proh-MAY-dee-oh)

avoid v. evitar (ay-vee-TAHR)

awful adj. terrible; horrible (tay-REE-blay; oh-REE-blay)

B

baby n. bebé; *Chi., Ec.* guagua (bay-BAY; GWAH-gwah)

bacon n. tocino (toh-SEE-noh)

bad adj. mal; malo (mahl; MAH-loh)

bag n. bolsa (BOHL-sah)

baggage n. equipaje (ay-key-PAH-hay)

bakery n. panadería (pah-nah-day-REE-ah)

banana n. plátano; *PR* guineo; *Ven.* cambur (PLAH-tah-noh; ghee-NAY-oh; cahm-BOOR)

bank n. banco (BAHN-coh)

bar n. bar (bahr)

barber n. barbero; *Arg., Mex., Uru.* peluquero (bahr-BAY-roh; pay-loo-KAY-roh)

bargain n. ganga v. regatear; *Chi.* pelear el precio (GAHN-gah; ray-gah-tay-AHR)

bargaining n. regateo (ray-gah-TAY-oh)

basis n. base (BAH-say)

basket n. canasta (cah-NAHS-tah)

bath n. baño (BAH-nyoh)

bathe v. bañar; bañar(se) (bah-NYARH; bah-NYAHR-say)

bathroom n. sala de baño; baño (SAH-lah day BAH-nyoh)

bathtub n. bañera; *Arg., Cuba* bañadera; *Mex.* tina (bah-NYAY-rah; bah-nyah-DAY-rah; TEE-nah)

battery n. batería; pila (bah-tay-REE-ah; PEE-lah)

be v. ser; estar (sayr; ays-TAHR)

be able v. poder (poh-DAYR)

beach n. playa (PLAH-yah)

be afraid v. tener miedo (tay-NAYR mee-AY-doh)

beak n. pico (PEE-coh)

beans (dry) n. *Arg., Bol., Chi., Ec., Uru.* porotos; *Cuba, Mex.* frijoles (poh-ROH-tohs; free-HOH-lays)

beautiful adj. hermoso; bello (ayr-MOH-soh; BAY-yoh)

beauty shop n. salón de belleza; peluquería (sah-LOHN day bay-YAY-sah; pay-loo-kay-REE-ah)

because conj. porque (POHR-kay)

bed n. cama (CAH-mah)

bedroom n. cuarto de dormir; *Arg., Chi.* pieza; *Cuba, Uru., Ven.* habitación; *Mex.* recámara; *Uru.* cuarto (KWAHR-toh de dohr-MEER; pee-AY-sah; ah-bee-tah-see-OHN; ray-CAH-mah-rah; KWAHR-toh)

beef n. carne de res (CAHR-nay day rays)

beefsteak n. bistec; *RP* bife (bees-TAYK; BEE-fay)

beer n. cerveza (sayr-VAY-sah)

beet n. remolacha; *Mex.* betabel (ray-moh-LAH-chah; bay-tah-BAYL)

before prep., adv. ante; conj. antes de que (AHN-tay; AHN-tays day kay)

beggar n. mendigo (mayn-DEE-goh)

begin v. empezar; comenzar (aym-pay-SAHR; coh-mayn-SAHR)

behind prep. adv. detrás (day-TRAHS)

be hungry v. tener hambre (tay-NAYR AHM-bray)

believe v. creer (cray-AYR)

bell n. timbre (TEEM-bray)

bellhop n. botones (boh-TOH-nays)

belong v. pertenecer (payr-tay-nay-SAYR)

below adv. debajo; prep. debajo de (day-BAH-hoh day)

belt n. cinturón (seen-too-ROHN)

be right v. tener razón (tay-NAYR rah-SOHN)

beside prep. al lado de (ahl LAH-doh day)

be sorry v. sentir(se) (sayn-TEER-say)

best adj. mejor (may-HOHR)

be thirsty v. tener sed (tay-NAYR sayd)

better adv. mejor (may-HOHR)

between prep. entre (AYN-tray)

beverage n. bebida (bay-BEE-dah)

be worth v. valer (vah-LAYR)

be wrong v. equivocar(se) (ah-kee-voh-CAHR-say)

bicycle n. bicicleta (bee-see-CLAY-tah)

big adj. grande (GRAHN-day)

bill n. cuenta; (money) billete (coo-AYN-tah; bee-YAY-tay)

bird n. pájaro (PAH-hah-roh)

birth n. nacimiento (nah-see-mee-AYN-toh)

birthday n. cumpleaños (coom-play-AHN-yohs)

black adj. negro (NAY-groh)

block n. cuadra (KWAH-drah)

blond n., adj. rubio; *Mex.* güero (ROO-bee-oh; GWAY-roh)

blouse n. blusa (BLOO-sah)

blue n., adj. azul (ah-SOOL)

boat n. barco (BAHR-coh)

bobby pin n. *Ec.* imperdible; *Mex., Uru.* pasador; *Pan.* gancho (eem-payr-DEE-blay; pah-sah-DOHR; GHAN-choh)

body n. cuerpo (coo-AYR-poh)

book n. libro (LEE-broh)

bookstore n. librería (lee-bray-REE-ah)

border n. frontera (frohn-TAY-rah)

bottle n. botella (boh-TAY-yah)

bowl n. *Arg., Bol., Mex.* tazón; *Ven.* taza (tah-SOHN; TAH-sah)

box n. caja (CAH-hah)

box office n. taquilla (tah-KEY-yah)

boy n. niño; muchacho (NEE-nyoh; moo-CHAH-choh)

boyfriend n. novio; *Ven.* empate (NOH-vee-oh; aym-PAH-tay)

bracelet n. pulsera; *Ven.* brazalete (pool-SAY-rah; brah-sah-LAY-tay)

branch n. sucursal (soo-coor-SAHL)

brand n. marca (MAHR-cah)

bread n. pan (pahn)

break v. romper (rohm-PAYR)

breakfast n. desayuno (day-sah-YOO-noh)

bridge n. puente (PWAYN-tay)

brief adj. breve (BRAY-vay)

bring v. traer (trah-AYR)

broad adj. ancho (AHN-choh)

broken adj. roto (ROH-toh)

brother n. hermano (ayr-MAH-noh)

brown adj. pardo; *Mex.* café (PAHR-doh; cah-FAY)

buddy n. *Arg., Bol., Uru.* compinche; *Cuba* socio; *Mex.* cuate (cohm-PEEN-chay; SOH-see-oh; KWAH-tay)

budget n. presupuesto (pray-soo-PWAYS-toh)

bug n. insecto; bicho (vulgar in *PR*) (een-SAYK-toh; BEE-choh)

bulb n. bombilla; *Mex.* foco (bohm-BEE-yah; FOH-coh)

burn v. quemar (kay-MAHR)

bus (city) n. *Arg., Bol.* colectivo; *Carib.* guagua; *Mex.* camión (coh-layk-TEE-voh; GWAH-gwah; cah-mee-OHN)

bus (intercity) n. *Caribe, Mex.* autobús (ah-oo-toh-BOOS)

business n. negocio (nay-GOH-see-oh)

business card n. tarjeta de presentación (tahr-HAY-tah day pray-sayn-tah-see-OHN)

businessman n. hombre de negocios (OHM-bray de nay-GOH-see-ohs)

bus stop n. parada; *Chi., Col.* paradero (pah-RAH-dah; par-rah-DAY-roh)

but conj. pero (PAY-roh)

butter n. mantequilla; *Arg.* manteca (mahn-tay-KEY-yah; mahn-TAY-cah)

button n. botón (boh-TOHN)

buy v. comprar (cohm-PRAHR)

buyer n. comprador (cohm-prah-DOHR)

by prep. por (pohr)

C

cab n. taxi; *Arg.* tacho; *Cuba* máquina (TAHK-see; TAH-choh)

cake n. *Chi., Ec., Uru.* torta; *Mex.* pastel; *PR* bizcocho (tohr-tah-pah-STAYL; bees-COH-choh)

calendar n. calendario (cah-layn-DAH-ree-oh)

call n. llamada; v. llamar (yah-MAH-dah; yah-MAHR)

camera n. cámara (CAH-mah-rah)

camp n. campamento (cahm-pah-MAYN-toh)

can n. lata; v. poder (LAH-tah; poh-DAYR)

candle n. vela (VAY-lah)

candy n. dulces (DOOL-says)

canyon n. cañón (cah-NYOHN)

capital n. capital (cah-pee-TAHL)

car n. auto; carro; coche (AH-oo-toh; CAH-roh; COH-chay)

carburetor n. carburador (cahr-boo-rah-DOHR)

card n. tarjeta (tahr-HAY-tah)

care for v. cuidar (coo-ee-DAHR)

careful adj. cuidadoso (coo-ee-dah-DOH-soh)

cargo n. carga; cargamento (CAHR-gah; cahr-gah-MAYN-toh)

carry v. llevar (yay-VAHR)

cart n. carreta (cah-RAY-tah)

case n. caso (KAH-soh)

cash n. efectivo (ay-FAYKT-tee-voh)

cashier n. cajero (cah-HAYR-roh)

cat n. gato (GAH-toh)

catch up v. alcanzar (ahl-cahn-SAHR)

cathedral n. catedral (cah-tay-DRAHL)

cause n. causa; v. causar (CAH-oo-sah; cah-oo-SAHR)

cave n. cueva (coo-AY-vah)

cellar n. sótano (SOH-tah-noh)

cent n. centavo (sayn-TAH-voh)

central adj. central (sayn-TRAHL)

central heating n. calefacción (cah-lay-fahk-see-OHN)

ceramics n. cerámica (say-RAH-mee-cah)

certainly adv. seguramente (say-goo-rah-MAYN-tay)

certificate n. certificado (sayr-tee-fee-CAH-doh)

chair n. silla (SEE-yah)

champagne n. champaña (chahm-APH-nyah)

change n. cambio; v. cambiar (CAHM-bee-oh; cahm-bee-AHR)

charge v. cobrar (coh-BRAHR)

cheap adj. barato (bah-RAH-toh)

check n. cheque (bank); cuenta (restaurant) (CHAY-kay; coo-AYN-tah)

cheese n. queso (KAY-soh)

chewing gum n. chicle (CHEE-clay)

chicken n. pollo (POH-yoh)

child n. niño; niña (fem.) (NEE-nyoh; NEE-nyah)

chilli n. chile; SA aji (CHEE-lay; ah-HEE)

chilli sauce n. salsa picante (SAHL-sah pee-CAHN-tay)

chocolate n. chocolate (choh-coh-LAH-tay)

choose v. escoger (ays-coh-HAYR)

chop n. chuleta (choo-LAY-tah)

Christmas n. Navidad (nah-vee-DAHD)

church n. iglesia (ee-GLAY-see-ah)

cigar n. *Cuba, Ven.* tabaco; *Ec., PR* cigarro; *Mex., Pe.* puro (tah-BAH-coh; see-GAH-roh; POO-roh)

cigarette n. cigarrillo; *Cuba, Mex.* cigarro (see-gah-REE-yoh; see-GAH-roh)

cinnamon n. canela (cah-NAY-lah)

circle n. círculo (SEER-coo-loh)

citizen n. ciudadano (see-oo-da-DAH-noh)

city n. ciudad (see-oo-DAHD)

city bus n. *Arg., Bol.* colectivo; *Carib.* guagua; *Mex.* camión (coh-layk-TEE-voh; GWAH-gwah; cah-mee-OHN)

claim n. reclamación; v. reclamar (ray-clah-mah-see-OHN; ray-clah-MAHR)

class n. clase (CLAH-say)

clean adj. limpio; v. limpiar (LEEM-pee-oh; leem-pee-AHR)

clerk n. dependiente; *Arg.* vendedor (day-payn-dee-AYN-tay; vayn-day-DOHR)

climate n. clima (CLEE-mah)

climb v. subir (soo-BEER)

clock n. reloj (ray-LOH)

close v. cerrar, (say-RAHR); adv. cerca (SAYR-cah)

cloth n. tela (TAY-lah)

clothes n. ropa (ROH-pah)

club n. club (cloob)

coffee n. café (cah-FAY)

cognac n. coñac (coh-NYAK)

coin n. moneda (moh-NAY-dah)

cold n., adj. frío (temperature); resfriado (FREE-oh; rays-free-AH-doh)

color n. color (coh-LOHR)

comb n. peine (PAY-nay)

come v. venir (vay-NEER)

come down v. bajar (bah-HAR)

Come in! imper. ¡Pase! (PAH-say)

come in v. entrar; pasar (ayn-TRAHR; pah-SAHR)

come out v. salir (sah-LEER)

comfortable adj. cómodo (COH-moh-doh)

commerce n. comercio (coh-MAYR-see-oh)

commercial adj. comercial (coh-mayr-see-AHL)

commission n. comisión (coh-mee-see-OHN)

companion n. compañero (cohm-pah-NYAY-roh)

company n. compañía (cohm-pah-NYEE-ah)

complain v. quejar(se) (kay-HAR-say)

complete adj. completo (cohm-PLAY-toh)

computer n. computadora (cohm-poo-tah-DOHR-ah)

concert n. concierto (cohn-see-AYR-toh)

conclusion n. conclusión (cohn-cloo-see-OHN)

condition n. condición (cohn-dee-see-OHN)

conference n. congreso (cohn-GRAY-soh)

congratulations n. felicitaciones (fay-lee-see-tah-see-OHN-ays)

congress n. congreso (legis.) (cohn-GRAY-soh)

consider v. considerar (cohn-see-day-RAHR)

consign v. consignar; entregar (cohn-seeg-NAHR; ayn-tray-GAHR)

consignment n. consignación (cohn-seeg-nah-see-OHN)

constant adj. constante (cohn-STAHN-tay)

constitute v. constituir (cohns-stee-too-EER)

consulate n. consulado (cohn-soo-LAH-doh)

consult v. consultar (cohn-sool-TAHR)

contact n. contacto (cohn-TAHK-toh)

contain v. contener (cohn-tay-NAYR)

container n. envase (ayn-VAH-say)

content adj. contento (cohn-TAYN-toh)

contents n. contenido (cohn-tay-NEE-doh)

continue v. continuar (cohn-tee-noo-AHR)

contract n. contrato (cohn-TRAH-toh)

control n. control; v. controlar (cohn-TROHL; cohn-troh-LAHR)

convenient adj. conveniente (cohn-vay-nee-AYN-tay)

converse v. conversar (cohn-vayr-SAHR)

cook n. cocinero; v. cocinar; guisar (coh-see-NAY-roh; coh-see-NAHR; ghee-SAHR)

cool adj. fresco (FRAYS-coh)

copy n. copia; v. copiar (COH-pee-ah; coh-pee-AHR)

corner n. esquina; rincón (ess-KEY-nah; reen-COHN)

corporation n. corporación (cohr-por-rah-see-OHN)

cost n. costo; precio; v. costar (COH-stoh; PRAY-see-oh; coh-STAHR)

cotton n. algodón (ahl-goh-DOHN)

count v. contar (cohn-TAHR)

country n. país (nation); campo (rural area) (pah-EES; CAHM-poh)

cover n. tapa; v. cubrir (TAH-pah; coo-BREER)

cracker n. galleta (gah-YAY-tah)

crash v. chocar (choh-CAHR)

crazy adj. loco (LOH-coh)

credit n. crédito (CRAY-dee-toh)

crime n. crimen (CREE-mayn)

cucumber n. pepino (pay-PEE-noh)

culture n. cultura (cool-TOO-rah)

cup n. taza (TAH-sah)

cure n. cura; v. curar (KOO-rah; koo-RAHR)

current adj. actual (ahk-too-AHL)

curtain n. cortina (cohr-TEE-nah)

curve n. curva (KOOR-vah)

custom duty n. derecho de aduana (day-RAY-choh de ah-DWAH-nah)

customer n. cliente (klee-AYN-tay)

customhouse n. aduana (ah-DWAH-nah)

cut v. cortar (cohr-TAHR)

D

daily adj. diario (dee-AH-ree-oh)

damage n. daño; v. dañar (DAH-nyoh; dah-NYAHR)

dance n. baile; v. bailar (BAH-ee-lay; bah-ee-LAHR)

danger n. peligro (pay-LEE-groh)

dangerous adj. peligroso (pay-lee-GROH-soh)

dark adj. oscuro (ohs-COO-roh)

date n. fecha; cita (FAY-chah; SEE-tah)

daughter n. hija (EE-hah)

day n. día (DEE-ah)

debt n. deuda (DAY-oo-dah)

December n. diciembre (dee-see-AYM-bray)

decision n. decisión (day-see-dee-OHN)

declare v. declarar (day-clah-RAHR)

deep adj. profundo (proh-FOON-doh)

delay n. retraso (ray-TRAH-soh)

delicious adj. delicioso; sabroso; rico (day-lee-see-OH-soh; sah-BROH-soh; REE-coh)

deliver v. entregar (ayn-tray-GAHR)

demand n. demanda; v. demandar (de-MAHN-dah; de-mahn-DAHR)

demonstrate v. demostrar (day-mohs-TRAHR)

dentist n. dentista (dayn-TEES-tah)

department n. departamento (day-pahr-tah-MAYN-toh)

department store n. almacén; tienda de departamentos (ahl-mah-SAYN; tee-AYN-day day day-pahr-tah-MAYN-tohs)

deposit n. depósito; v. depositar (day-POH-see-toh; day-poh-see-TAHR)

describe v. describir (days-cree-VEER)

description n. descripción (days-creep-see-OHN)

dessert n. postre (POHS-tray)

detail n. detalle (day-TAH-yay)

determine v. determinar (day-tayr-mee-NAHR)

develop v. desarrollar; revelar (photo) (days-ah-roh-YAHR; ray-vay-LAHR)

diamond n. diamante (dee-ah-MAHN-tay)

die v. morir (moh-REER)

difference n. diferencia (dee-fay-RAYN-see-ah)

different adj. diferente (dee-fay-RAYN-tay)

dining room n. comedor (coh-may-DOHR)

dinner n. cena; comida (SAY-nah; coh-MEE-dah)

direct adj. directo; v. dirigir (dee-RAYK-toh; dee-ree-HEER)

direction n. dirección (dee-rayk-see-OHN)

director n. director (dee-rayk-TOHR)

dirt n. suciedad; *Arg.* roña (soo-see-ay-DAHD; ROH-nyah)

dirty adj. sucio (SOO-see-oh)

discount n. descuento (days-coo-AYN-toh)

discover v. descubrir (days-coo-BREER)

dish n. plato (PLAH-toh)

distance n. distancia (dees-TAHN-see-ah)

distant adj. distante (dees-TAHN-tay)

distribute v. distribuir (dees-tree-boo-EER)

disturb v. molestar (moh-lays-TAHR)

division n. división (dee-vee-see-OHN)

do v. hacer (ah-SAYR)

doctor n. médico; doctor (MAY-dee-coh; dohk-TOHR)

document n. documento (doh-coo-MAYN-toh)

dog n. perro (PAY-roh)

dollar n. dólar (DOH-lahr)

door n. puerta (PWAYR-tah)

double adj. doble (DOH-blay)

doubt n. duda; v. dudar (DOO-dah; doo-DAHR)

dozen n. docena (doh-SAY-nah)

drawer n. cajón (cah-HOHN)

dress n. vestido; v. vestir (vays-TEE-doh; vays-TEER)

drink n. bebida; *Mex.* copa; v. beber; tomar (bay-BEE-dah; COH-pah; bay-BAYR; toh-MAHR)

drive v. manejar; conducir (mah-nay-HAHR; cohn-doo-SEER)

driver n. chofer (choh-FAYR)

drug n. medicamento (may-dee-cah-MAYN-toh)

drugstore n. farmacia; *Cuba* botica (fahr-MAH-see-ah; boh-TEE-cah)

drunk n., adj. borracho (boh-RAH-choh)

dry adj. seco; v. secar (SAY-coh; say-CAHR)

due adj. debido; vencido (day-BEE-doh; vayn-SEE-doh)

during prep. durante (doo-RAHN-tay)

E

each pron., adj. cáda (CAH-dah)

early adv. temprano (taym-PRAH-noh)

earn v. ganar (gah-NAHR)

earnings n. ganancias (gah-NAHN-see-ahs)

earrings n. aretes; pendientes; *Arg.*, *Chi.*, aros (ah-RAY-tays; payn-dee-AYN-tays; AH-rohs)

earthquake n. temblor (taym-BLOHR)

easily adv. fácilmente (FAH-seel-mayn-tay)

east n. este (ESS-tay)

easy adj. fácil (FAH-seel)

eat v. comer (coh-MAYR)

economy n. economía (ay-coh-noh-MEE-ah)

efficient adj. eficiente (ay-fee-see-AYN-tay)

egg n. huevo; *Mex.* blanquillo (WAY-voh; blahn-KEY-yoh)

eight n., adj. ocho (OH-choh)

eighteen n., adj. diez y ocho (dee-AYS ee OH-choh)

eighty n., adj. ochenta (oh-CHAYN-tah)

element n. elemento (ay-lay-MAYN-toh)

elevator n. elevador; *SA* ascensor (ay-lay-vah-DOHR; ah-sayn-SOHR)

eleven n., adj. once (OHN-say)

embassy n. embajada (aym-bah-HAH-dah)

embrace n. abrazo; v. abrazar(se) (ah-BRAH-soh; ah-brah-SAHR-say)

emerald n. esmeralda (ess-may-RAHL-dah)

employ v. emplear (aym-play-AHR)

employment n. empleo (aym-PLAY-oh)

empty adj. vacío (vah-SEE-oh)

encounter n. encuentro; v. encontrar (ayn-coo-AYN-troh; ayn-cohn-TRAHR)

end n. fin; v. terminar (feen; tayr-mee-NAHR)

engine n. motor (moh-TOHR)

enough adj., adv. bastante (bah-STAHN-tay)

enter v. entrar (ayn-TRAHR)

enterprise n. empresa (aym-PRAY-sah)

entertainment n. diversión (dee-vayr-see-OHN)

entire adj. entero (ayn-TAY-roh)

entrance n. entrada (ayn-TRAH-dah)

envelope n. sobre (SOH-bray)

equal adj. igual (ee-GWAL)

erase v. borrar (boh-RAHR)

especially adv. especialmente (ays-pay-see-ahl-MAYN-tay)

establish v. establecer (ays-tah-blay-SAYR)

estimate n. presupuesto (pray-soo-PWAY-stoh)

even adv. aún (ah-OON)

evening n. tarde; noche (TAHR-day; NOH-chay)

every adj. todo; cada uno (TOH-doh; CAH-dah OO-noh)

everybody pron. todo el mundo (TOH-doh el MOON-doh)

everything pron. todo (TOH-doh)

everywhere adv. en todas partes (ayn TOH-dahs PAHR-tays)

examination n. examen (ex-AH-mayn)

examine v. examinar (ex-ah-mee-NAHR)

example n. ejemplo (ay-HAYM-ploh)

excellent adj. excelente (ex-say-LAYN-tay)

excess n., adj. exceso (ex-SAY-soh)

exchange n. cambio; v. cambiar (CAHM-bee-oh; cahm-bee-AHR)

excursion n. excursión (ex-coor-see-OHN)

excuse v. perdonar (payr-doh-NAHR)

exhibition n. exhibición (ex-ee-bee-see-OHN)

exit n. salida (sah-LEE-dah)

expect v. esperar (ess-pay-RAHR)

expense n. gasto (GAHS-toh)

expensive adj. caro (CAH-roh)

explain v. explicar (ex-plee-CAHR)

explanation n. explicación (ex-plee-cah-see-OHN)

export v. exportar (ex-pohr-TAHR)

exports n. exportaciones (ex-pohr-tah-see-OHN-ays)

exterior n. exterior; adj. exterior (ex-tay-ree-OHR)

extremely adv. sumamente (soo-mah-MAYN-tay)

eye n. ojo (OH-hoh)

eyeglasses n. anteojos; *Mex.* lentes; *Cuba* espejuelos (ahn-tay-OH-hohs; LAYN-tays; ess-pay-hoo-AY-lohs)

F

fabric n. tela (TAY-lah)

face n. cara (CAH-rah)

fact n. hecho (AY-choh)

factory n. fábrica (FAH-bree-cah)

fail v. fracasar (frah-cah-SAHR)

failure n. fracaso (frah-CAH-soh)

fall n. otoño; v. caer(se) (oh-TOH-nyoh; cah-AYR-say)

family n. familia (fah-MEE-lee-ah)

famous adj. famoso (fah-MOH-soh)

fantastic adj. fantástico (fahn-TAHS-tee-coh)

far adv. lejos (LAY-hohs)

fare n. tarifa (tah-REE-fah)

farm n. granja; *Cuba* finca; *RP* estancia (GRAHN-hah; FEEN-cah; ess-TAHN-see-ah)

fast adj. rápido (RAH-pee-doh)

fat adj. gordo (GOHR-doh)

father n. padre (PAH-dray)

fear n. miedo; v. tener miedo (mee-AY-doh; tay-NAYR mee-AY-doh)

February n. febrero (fay-BRAY-roh)

fee n. honorario (oh-noh-RAH-ree-oh)

feel v. sentir(se) (sayn-TEER-say)

fever n. fiebre; *Mex.* calentura (fee-AY-bray; cah-LAYN-too-rah)

few adj. pocos; algunos (POH-cohs; ahl-GOO-nohs)

fifteen n., adj. quince (KEYN-say)

fifty n., adj. cincuenta (seen-KWAYN-tah)

fight n. lucha; v. luchar (LOO-chah; loo-CHAHR)

file n. archivo (for papers); v. archivar (papers) (ahr-CHEE-voh; ahr-chee-VAHR)

film n. película (pay-LEE-coo-lah)

finance n. finanza; v. financiar (fee-NAHN-sah; fee-nahn-see-AHR)

find v. encontrar (ayn-cohn-TRAHR)

Fine! interj. ¡Muy bien! (MOO-ee bee-AYN)

finger n. dedo (DAY-doh)

finish v. terminar (tayr-mee-NAHR)

fire n. fuego; *Cuba, Ven.* candela (FWAY-goh; cahn-DAY-lah)

first n., adj., adv. primero (pree-MAY-roh)

fish n. pescado (pays-CAH-doh)

fishing n. pesca (PAYS-cah)

five n., adj. cinco (SEE-coh)

fix v. arreglar (ahr-ray-GLAHR)

flag n. bandera (bahn-DAY-rah)

flight n. vuelo (VWAY-loh)

floor n. piso (PEE-soh)

flower n. flor (flohr)

flu n. gripe; *Mex.* gripa (GREE-pay; GREE-pah)

fly v. volar (voh-LAHR)

follow v. seguir (say-GHEER)

food n. comida (coh-MEE-dah)

foot n. pie (pee-AY)

football (Amer.) n. fútbol (FOOT-bohl)

for prep. por; para (pohr; PAH-rah)

foreign adj. extranjero (ex-trahn-HAY-roh)

forget v. olvidar(se) (ohl-vee-DAHR-say)

fork n. tenedor; *Andes, Mex.* trinche (tay-nay-DOHR; TREEN-chay)

form n. forma; v. formar (FOHR-mah; fohr-MAHR)

forty n., adj. cuarenta (kwah-RAYN-tah)

four n., adj. cuatro (KWAH-troh)

fourteen n., adj. catorce (cah-TOHR-say)

free adj. libre; adv. gratis (free of charge) (LEE-bray; GRAH-tees)

freedom n. libertad (lee-bayr-TAHD)

freight n. carga; flete (CAHR-gah; FLAY-tay)

frequently adv. frecuentemente (fray-kwayn-tay-MAYN-tay)

fresh adj. fresco (FRAYS-coh)

Friday n. viernes (vee-AYR-nays)

friend n. amigo (ah-MEE-goh)

from prep. de; desde (day; DAYS-day)

fruit n. fruta (FROO-tah)

full adj. lleno (YAY-noh)

fund n. fondo (FOHN-doh)

funny adj. cómico (COH-mee-coh)

furniture n. muebles (moo-AY-blays)

future n. futuro (foo-TOO-roh)

G

gallon n. galón (gah-LOHN)

gamble v. jugar (hoo-GAHR)

gambling n. juego (HWAY-goh)

game n. juego (HWAY-goh)

garage n. garaje; *Mex.* cochera (gah-RAH-hay; coh-CHAY-rah)

garbage n. basura (bah-SOO-rah)

garden n. jardín (hahr-DEEN)

garlic n. ajo (AH-hoh)

gas n. gasolina; *Arg.* nafta (gah-soh-LEE-nah; NAHF-tah)

gem n. joya (HOH-yah)

general n. (mil.) general; adj. general (hay-nay-RAHL)

gentleman n. caballero; señor (cah-bah-YAY-roh; say-NYOHR)

genuine adj. genuino (hay-noo-EE-noh)

get v. obtener (ohb-tay-NAYR)

gift n. regalo (ray-GAH-loh)

gin n. ginebra (hee-NAY-brah)

girl n. muchacha; niña (moo-CHAH-chah; NEE-nyah)

girlfriend n. novia; *Ven.* empate (NOH-vee-ah; aym-PAH-tay)

give v. dar (dahr)

glass n. vaso (tumbler) (VAH-soh)

glasses n. anteojos; lentes; *Cuba* espejuelos (ahn-tay-OH-hohs; LAYN-tays; ess-pay-hoo-AY-lohs)

glove n. guante (GWAN-tay)

glue n. pegamento; *Cuba, Uru.* goma (pay-gah-MAYN-toh; GOH-mah)

go v. ir (eer)

go away v. ir(se) (EER-say)

go back v. regresar (ray-gray-SAHR)

god n. dios (dee-OHS)

gold n. oro (OH-roh)

golf n. golf (golf)

good adj. bueno (BWAY-noh)

good-bye n. adiós (ah-dee-OHS)

goods n. mercancías (mayr-cahn-SEE-ahs)

go out v. salir (sah-LEER)

go shopping v. ir de compras (eer day COHM-prahs)

government n. gobierno (goh-bee-AYR-noh)

governor n. gobernador (goh-bayr-nah-DOHR)

grandfather n. abuelo (ah-BWAY-loh)

grandmother n. abuela (ah-BWAY-lah)

grandson n. nieto (nee-AY-toh)

grape n. uva (OO-vah)

grapefruit n. toronja; *Arg.* pomelo (toh-ROHN-hah; poh-MAY-loh)

gravy n. salsa (SAHL-sah)

gray n., adj. gris (grees)

great adj. gran; grande (grahn; GRAHN-day)

great deal adj., adv. mucho (MOO-choh)

green n., adj. verde (VAHR-day)

greet v. saludar (sah-loo-DAHR)

greeting n. saludo (sah-LOO-doh)

grocery n. *Cuba, PR, Ven.* bodega; *Mex.* abarrotes (boh-DAY-gah; ah-bah-ROH-tays)

ground floor n. piso bajo; *Mex.* planta baja (PEE-soh BAH-hoh; PLAHN-tah BAH-hah)

group n. grupo (GROO-poh)

guarantee v. garantizar (gah-rahn-tee-SAHR)

guaranty n. garantía (gah-rahn-TEE-ah)

guest n. invitado (een-vee-TAH-doh)

guide n. guía (GHEE-ah)

guidebook n. guía (GHEE-ah)

guitar n. guitarra (ghee-TAH-rah)

gulf n. golfo (GOHL-foh)

gum n. goma; chicle (GOH-mah; CHEE-clay)

gun n. fusil (foo-SEEL)

gymnasium n. gimnasio (heem-NAH-see-oh)

H

hair n. pelo (PAY-loh)

hairdresser n. peluquero (pay-loo-KAY-roh)

half adj. medio (MAY-dee-oh)

hall n. pasillo (pah-SEE-yoh)

ham n. jamón (hah-MOHN)

hamburger n. hamburguesa (ahm-boor-GAY-sah)

hand n. mano (MAH-noh)

handbag n. cartera; *Ec.* bolso; *Mex.* bolsa (cahr-TAY-rah; BOHL-soh; BOHL-sah)

handle n. manija (mah-NEE-hah)

handrail n. pasamanos (pah-sah-MAH-nohs)

handsome adj. guapo; bello; *Uru.* bien parecido (GWAH-poh; BAY-yoh; bee-AYN pah-ray-SEE-doh)

hanger n. colgador; *Mex.* gancho; *Cuba* perchero (cohl-gah-DOHR; GAHN-choh; payr-CHAY-roh)

happen v. pasar (pah-SAHR)

happy adj. feliz (fay-LEES)

hard adj. duro; difícil (DOO-roh; dee-FEE-seel)

hardware store n. ferretería (fay-ray-tay-REE-ah)

harm n. daño; v. dañar (DAH-nyoh; dah-NYAHR)

hat n. sombrero (sohm-BRAY-roh)

hate n. odio; v. odiar (OH-dee-oh; oh-dee-AHR)

have v. tener (tay-NAYR)

have fun v. divertir(se) (dee-vayr-TEER-say)

he pron. él (ayl)

head n. cabeza (cah-BAY-sah)

headache n. dolor de cabeza (doh-LOHR de cah-BAY-sah)

health n. salud (sah-LOOD)

healthy adj. saludable; sano (sah-loo-DAH-blay; SAH-noh)

hear v. oír; escuchar (oh-EER; ess-coo-CHAHR)

heart n. corazón (coh-rah-SOHN)

heat n. calor (cah-LOHR)

heaven n. cielo (see-AY-loh)

heavy adj. pesado (pay-SAH-doh)

heel n. tacón (shoe) (tah-COHN)

height n. altura (ahl-TOO-rah)

Help! interj. ¡Socorro! (soh-COH-roh)

here adv. aquí (ah-KEY)

hide v. esconder (ess-cohn-DAYR)

highway n. carretera (cah-ray-TAY-rah)

hire v. alquilar (ahl-key-LAHR)

hole n. agujero; hueco (ah-goo-HAY-roh; WAY-coh)

holiday n. día festivo (DEE-ah fays-TEE-voh)

home n. hogar; adv. a casa; en casa (oh-GAHR; ah CAH-sah; ayn CAH-sah)

homeland n. patria (PAH-tree-ah)

honest adj. honesto (oh-NAYS-toh)

honeymoon n. luna de miel (LOO-nah day mee-AYL)

hope n. esperanza; v. esperar (ess-pay-RAHN-sah; ess-pay-RAHR)

hors d'oeuvres n. entremeses; *Mex*. botanas (ayn-tray-MAY-says; boh-TAH-nahs)

horse n. caballo (cah-BAH-yoh)

hospital n. hospital (ohs-pee-TAHL)

hot adj. caliente; picante (spicy) (cah-lee-AYN-tay; pee-CAHN-tay)

hot-dog n. perro caliente (PAY-roh cah-lee-AYN-tay)

hotel n. hotel (oh-TAYL)

hour n. hora (OH-rah)

house n. casa (CAH-sah)

how adv. como (COH-moh)

however conj. sin embargo (seen aym-BAHR-goh)

how many? ¿cuántos? (KWAN-tohs)

how much? ¿cuánto? (KWAN-toh)

how soon? ¿cuándo? (KWAN-doh)

hundred n., adj. cien; ciento (see-AYN; see-AYN-toh)

hunger n. hambre (AHM-bray)

hunt v. cazar (cah-SAHR)

hurry v. ir de prisa (eer day PREE-sah)

husband n. esposo; marido (ess-POH-soh; mah-REE-doh)

I

I pron. yo (yoh)

ice n. hielo (ee-AY-loh)

ice cream n. helado; *PR* mantecado (ay-LAH-doh; mahn-tay-CAH-doh)

idea n. idea (ee-DAY-ah)

identity card n. cédula (de identidad) (SAY-doo-lah de ee-dayn-tee-TAHD)

if conj. si (see)

ill adj. enfermo (ayn-FAYR-moh)

illegal adj. ilegal (ee-lay-GAHL)

image n. imagen (ee-MAH-hen)

imagine v. imaginar (ee-mah-hee-NAHR)

immediately adv. en seguida; *Mex.* ahorita (ayn say-GHEE-dah; ah-oh-REE-tah)

immigrant n. inmigrante (een-mee-GRAHN-tay)

import v. importar (eem-pohr-TAHR)

importance n. importancia (eem-pohr-TAHN-see-ah)

important adj. importante (eem-pohr-TAHN-tay)

importer n. importador (eem-pohr-tah-DOHR)

imports n. importaciones (eem-pohr-tah-see-OH-nays)

impossible adj. imposible (eem-pohs-SEE-blay)

impress v. impresionar (eem-pray-see-oh-NAHR)

impressive adj. impresionante (eem-pray-see-oh-NAHN-tay)

improve v. mejorar (may-hoh-RAHR)

in prep. en (ayn)

in advance adv. por adelantado (pohr ah-day-lahn-TAH-doh)

in case conj. en caso (ayn CAH-soh)

inch n. pulgada (pool-GAH-dah)

include v. incluir (een-cloo-EER)

including prep. incluso (een-CLOO-soh)

income n. ingreso (een-GRAY-soh)

income tax n. impuesto de utilidades (eem-PWAYS-toh day oo-tee-lee-DAH-days)

increase v. aumentar (ay-oo-mayn-TAHR)

independent adj. independiente (een-day-payn-dee-AYN-tay)

indicate v. indicar (een-dee-CAHR)

industry n. industria (een-DOOS-tree-ah)

inexpensive adj. barato (bah-RAH-toh)

inferior adj. inferior (een-fay-ree-OHR)

inside adv. adentro (ah-DAYN-troh)

insist v. insistir (een-see-STEER)

inspect v. inspeccionar (een-spayk-see-oh-NAHR)

instead of prep. en vez de (ayn vays day)

institute n. instituto (een-stee-TOO-toh)

instruction n. instrucción (een-strook-see-OHN)

insult v. insultar (een-sool-TAHR)

insurance n. seguro (say-GOO-roh)

insure v. asegurar (ay-say-goo-RAHR)

intelligent adj. inteligente (een-tay-lee-HAYN-tay)

intercity bus n. *Arg.* micro; *Carib.*, *Mex.* autobús; *Pe.*, *Uru.* ómnibus (MEE-croh; ah-oo-toh-BOOS; OHM-nee-boos)

interpreter n. intérprete (een-TAYR-pray-tay)

into prep. en; adentro (ayn; ah-DAYN-troh)

introduce v. presentar (pray-sayn-TAHR)

invitation n. invitación (een-vee-tah-see-OHN)

invite v. invitar (een-vee-TAHR)

iron n. plancha; v. planchar (PLAHN-chah; plahn-CHAHR)

island n. isla (EES-lah)

item n. artículo (ahr-TEE-coo-loh)

J

jacket n. chaqueta; *Mex.* chamarra; *Pe.* casaca (chah-KAY-tah; chah-MAH-rah; cah-SAH-cah)

jail n. cárcel (CAHR-sayl)

jam n. mermelada (mayr-may-LAH-dah)

January n. enero (ay-NAY-roh)

jellyfish n. *Bol.*, *Uru.* medusa; *Cuba*, *Mex.* aguamala (may-DOO-sah; ah-gwah-MAH-lah)

jewel n. joya (HOH-yah)

jewelry n. joyería (hoh-yay-REE-ah)

job n. empleo (aym-PLAY-oh)

joke n. broma; chiste (BROH-mah; CHEES-tay)

juice n. jugo; *CR* zumo (HOO-goh; SOO-moh)

July n. julio (HOO-lee-oh)

jump v. saltar; *Mex.* brincar (sahl-TAHR; breen-CAHR)

jungle n. selva (SAYL-vah)

June n. junio (HOO-nee-oh)

justice n. justicia (hoos-TEE-see-ah)

K

keep v. mantener (mahn-tay-NAYR)

key n. llave (YAH-vay)

kid n. *Cuba, Pe.* chico; *Mex.* chamaco (CHEE-coh; chah-MAH-coh)

kill v. matar (mah-TAHR)

kilogram n. kilo(gramo) (key-loh-GRAH-moh)

kilometer n. kilómetro (key-LOH-may-troh)

kind adj. bondadoso (bohn-dah-DOH-soh)

kiss n. beso; v. besar (BAY-soh; bay-SAHR)

kitchen n. cocina (coh-SEE-nah)

knee n. rodilla (roh-DEE-yah)

knife n. cuchillo (coo-CHEE-yoh)

knock v. tocar (toh-CAHR)

know v. saber; conocer (sah-BAYR; coh-noh-SAYR)

know how v. saber (say-BAYR)

knowledge n. conocimiento (coh-noh-see-mee-AYN-toh)

L

label n. etiqueta (ay-tee-KAY-tah)

lace n. encaje (ayn-CAH-hay)

lack n. falta; v. faltar (FAHL-tah; fahl-TAHR)

lady n. señora; dama (say-NYOHR-ah; DAH-mah)

lake n. lago (LAH-goh)

lamp n. lámpara (LAHM-pah-rah)

land n. tierra; v. aterrizar (tee-AY-rah; ah-tay-ree-SAHR)

landscape n. paisaje (pah-ee-SAH-hay)

language n. idioma (ee-dee-OH-mah)

large adj. grande (GRAHN-day)

last adj. ultimo (OOL-tee-moh)

last name n. apellido (ah-pay-YEE-doh)

late adv. tarde (TAHR-day)

laugh n. risa; v. reír(se) (REE-sah; ray-EER-say)

laundry n. lavandería (lah-vahn-day-REE-ah)

law n. ley (lay)

lawyer n. abogado; *Mex.* licenciado (ah-boh-GAH-doh; lee-sayn-see-AH-doh)

lazy adj. flojo; *Cuba* vago (FLOH-hoh; VAH-goh)

leader n. dirigente (dee-ree-HAYN-tay)

learn v. aprender (ah-prayn-DAYR)

least adj. menor (may-NOHR)

leather n. cuero (coo-AY-roh)

leave v. salir (sah-LEER)

leave out v. omitir (oh-mee-TEER)

left adj. izquierdo (ees-key-AHR-doh)

leg n. pierna (pee-AYR-nah)

legal adj. legal (lay-GAHL)

lemon n. limón (lee-MOHN)

lemonade n. limonada (lee-moh-NAH-dah)

lend v. prestar (prays-TAHR)

length n. largo (LAHR-goh)

lens n. lente (LAYN-tay)

less adj., adv. menos (MAY-nohs)

letter n. carta (CAHR-tah)

lettuce n. lechuga (lay-CHOO-gah)

library n. biblioteca (bee-blee-oh-TAY-cah)

license (driver's) n. *Arg.* permiso de manejo; *Mex.* licencia (de conducir) (payr-MEE-soh day mah-NAY-hoh; lee-SAYN-see-ah day cohn-doo-SEER)

lie n. mentira (mayn-TEE-rah)

life n. vida (VEE-dah)

life insurance n. seguro de vida (say-GOO-roh day VEE-dah)

lift v. levantar (lay-vahn-TAHR)

light n. luz (loos)

light bulb n. bombilla; *Arg.* lamparita; *Mex.* foco (bohm-BEE-yah; lahm-pah-REE-tah; FOH-coh)

like v. gustar (goos-TAHR)

lime n. limón (lee-MOHN)

liquor n. licor (lee-COHR)

list n. lista (LEES-tah)

listen v. escuchar (ess-coo-CHAHR)

little adj., adv. poco; pequeño; chico (POH-coh; pay-KAY-nyoh; CHEE-coh)

live v. vivir (vee-VEEHR)

living room n. sala (SAH-lah)

lobster n. langosta (lahn-GHOHS-tah)

long adj. largo (LAHR-goh)

look at v. mirar (mee-RAHR)

look for v. buscar (boos-CAHR)

lose v. perder (payr-DAYHR)

lottery n. lotería (loh-tay-REE-ah)

loud adj. alto; fuerte (AHL-toh; FWAR-tay)

love n. amor; v. amar; querer (ah-MOHR; ah-MAHR; kay-RAYR)

luck n. suerte (SWAYR-tay)

luggage n. equipaje (ay-key-PAH-hay)

lunch (midday meal) n. *Bol.*, *Cuba*, *Ven.* almuerzo, *Mex.* comida (ahl-moo-AYR-soh; coh-MEE-dah)

luxury n. lujo (LOO-hoh)

M

machine n. máquina (MAH-key-nah)

magazine n. revista (ray-VEES-tah)

maid n. criada; *Bol.*, *Ec.*, *Pan.* empleada; *Mex.*, *Uru.* sirvienta (cree-AH-dah; aym-play-AH-dah; seer-vee-AYN-tah)

mail n. correo; v. echar al correo (coh-RAY-oh; ay-CHAHR ahl coh-RAY-oh)

main adj. principal (preen-see-PAHL)

main square n. plaza mayor; *Mex.* zócalo (PLAH-sah mah-YOHR; SOH-cah-loh)

make v. hacer (ah-SAYR)

make a mistake v. equivocar(se) (ay-key-voh-CAHR-say)

man n. hombre (OHM-bray)

manager n. gerente (hay-RAHN-tay)

many adj. muchos (MOO-chohs)

map n. mapa (MAH-pah)

March n. marzo (MAHR-soh)

market n. mercado (mayr-CAH-doh)

married adj. casado (cah-SAH-doh)

match n. fósforo; *Mex.* cerillo (FOHS-foh-roh; say-REE-yoh)

May n. mayo (MAH-yoh)

me pron. me; a mí (may; ah mee)

meal n. comida (coh-MEE-dah)

meat n. carne (CAHR-nay)

meet v. conocer; encontrar (coh-noh-SAYR; ayn-cohn-TRAHR)

meeting n. reunión (ray-oo-nee-OHN)

melon n. melón (may-LOHN)

merchandise n. mercancía (mayr-cahn-SEE-ah)

message n. recado (ray-CAH-doh)

meter n. metro (MAY-troh)

mile n. milla (MEE-yah)

milk n. leche (LAY-chay)

million n. millón (mee-YOHN)

minute n. minuto (mee-NOO-toh)

Miss n. señorita (say-nyohr-REE-tah)

mistake n. error (ay-ROHR)

moment n. momento (moh-MAYN-toh)

Monday n. lunes (LOO-nays)

money n. dinero (dee-NAY-roh)

money order n. giro; *Ven.* orden de pago (HEE-roh; OHR-dayn day PAH-goh)

month n. mes (mays)

more adj., adv. más (mahs)

morning n. mañana (mah-NYAH-nah)

mosquito n. mosquito (mohs-KEY-toh)

most n. la major parte (de) (lah mah-YOHR PAHR-tay day)

mother n. madre; *Mex.* mamá (MAH-dray; mah-MAH)

motor n. motor (moh-TOHR)

motorcycle n. motocicleta (moh-toh-see-CLAY-tah)

mountain n. montaña (mohn-TAH-nyah)

mouth n. boca (BOH-cah)

Mr. n. señor (say-NYOR)

Mrs. n. señora (say-NYOH-rah)

much adj., adv. mucho (MOO-choh)

museum n. museo (moo-SAY-oh)

music n. música (MOO-see-cah)

must v. tener que (tay-NAHR kay)

my adj. mi; mío (mee; MEE-oh)

N

name n. nombre (NOHM-bray)

nap n. siesta (see-AYS-tah)

napkin n. servilleta (sayr-vee-YAY-tah)

nation n. nación (nah-see-OHN)

national adj. nacional (nah-see-oh-NAHL)

near adv. cerca; prep. cerca de (SAYR-cah day)

necessary adj. necesario (nay-say-SAHR-ee-oh)

neck n. cuello (coo-AY-yoh)

need v. necesitar (nay-say-see-TAHR)

neither adj. ninguno; conj. ni (neen-GOO-noh; nee)

never adv. nunca (NOON-cah)

nevertheless adv. sin embargo (seen aym-BAHR-goh)

new adj. nuevo (noo-AY-voh)

news n. noticias (noh-TEE-see-ahs)

newspaper n. periódico (pay-ree-OH-dee-coh)

next adj. próximo (PROCK-see-moh)

nice adj. simpático (seem-PAH-tee-coh)

night n. noche (NOH-chay)

nine n., adj. nueve (noo-AY-vay)

nineteen n., adj. diez y nueve (dee-AYS ee noo-AY-vay)

ninety n., adj. noventa (noh-VAYN-tah)

no adj. ninguno; adv. no (neen-GOO-noh; noh)

nobody pron. nadie (NAH-dee-ay)

noise n. ruido (roo-EE-doh)

noon n. mediodía (may-dee-oh-DEE-ah)

nor conj. ni (nee)

north n. norte (NOHR-tay)

nose n. nariz (nahr-EES)

note n. nota; v. notar (NOH-tah; noh-TAHR)

nothing pron. nada (NAH-dah)

November n. noviembre (noh-vee-AYM-bray)

now adv. ahora (ah-OH-rah)

number n. número (NOO-may-roh)

nurse n. enfermera (ayn-fayr-MAY-rah)

O

observe v. observar (ohb-sayr-VAHR)

obtain v. obtener (ohb-tay-NAYR)

occasionally adv. de vez en cuando (day vays ayn KWAN-doh)

occupation n. ocupación (oh-coo-pah-see-OHN)

occupy v. ocupar (oh-coo-PAHR)

occur v. ocurrir (oh-coo-REER)

October n. octubre (ok-TOO-bray)

of prep. de (day)

offer n. ofrecimiento; ofrecer (oh-fray-see-mee-AYN-toh; oh-fray-SAYR)

office n. oficina; *Arg., Ec., Pe.* (leg.); *Mex.* (leg.) bufete; (med.) consultorio (oh-fee-SEE-nah; boo-FAY-tay; cohn-sool-TOH-ree-oh)

officer n. oficial (oh-fee-see-AHL)

official n., adj. oficial (oh-fee-see-AHL)

often adv. frecuentemente (fray-kwayn-tay-MAYN-tay)

oil n. aceite (ah-SAY-tay)

old adj. viejo (vee-AY-hoh)

olive n. aceituna (ah-say-TOO-nah)

omelet n. *Cuba* tortilla (tohr-TEE-yah)

omit v. omitir (oh-mee-TEER)

on prep. en; sobre (ayn; SOH-bray)

once adv. una vez (OO-nah vays)

once more adv. otra vez (OH-trah vays)

one adj. un; una (oon; OO-nah)

onion n. cebolla (say-BOH-yah)

only adj. sólo; adv. solamente (SOH-loh; soh-lah-MAYN-tay)

open adj. abierto; v. abrir (ah-bee-AYR-toh; ah-BREER)

opportunity n. oportunidad (oh-pohr-too-nee-DAHD)

or conj. o (oh)

orange n. naranja (nah-RAHN-hah)

orange juice n. jugo de naranja; *PR* jugo de china (HOO-goh day nah-RAHN-hah; HOO-goh day CHEE-nah)

order n. orden; v. pedir (OHR-dayn; pay-DEER)

organization n. organización (ohr-gah-nee-sah-see-OHN)

organize v. organizar (ohr-gah-nee-SAHR)

other adj., pron. otro (OH-troh)

ounce n. onza (OHN-sah)

our adj. nuestro (noo-AYS-troh)

out adv. fuera (FWAY-rah)

outlet n. (elect.) toma-corriente; *Mex.* contacto (TOH-mah coh-ree-AYN-tay; cohn-TAYK-toh)

over prep. sobre (SOH-bray)

overweight n. sobrepeso (soh-bray-PAY-soh)

owe v. deber (day-BAYR)

owner n. dueño (doo-AY-nyoh)

P

package n. paquete (pah-KAY-tay)

page n. página (PAH-hee-nah)

pain n. dolor (doh-LOHR)

painter n. pintor (peen-TOHR)

pair n. pareja (couple); par (pah-RAY-hah; pahr)

pajamas n. pijamas (pee-CHAH-mahs)

pants n. pantalones; *Mex.* pantalón (pahn-tah-LOH-nays; pahn-tah-LOHN)

paper n. papel (pah-PAYL)

pardon n. perdón (payr-DOHN)

park n. parque; v. estacionar, *Cuba* parquear (PAHR-kay; ess-tah-see-oh-NAHR; pahr-kay-AHR)

parking n. estacionamiento; *Bol., Cuba* parqueo (ays-tah-see-oh-nah-mee-AYN-toh; pahr-KAY-oh)

part n. parte (PAHR-tay)

participate v. participar (pahr-tee-see-PAHR)

party n. fiesta; (pol.) partido (fee-AYS-tah)

pass n. pase; v. pasar (PAH-say; pah-SAHR)

passenger n. pasajero (pah-sah-HAY-roh)

passport n. pasaporte (pah-sah-POHR-tay)

past n., adj. pasado (pah-SAH-doh)

pay v. pagar (pay-GAHR)

payment n. pago (PAH-goh)

peach n. melocotón; *Arg., Mex., Pan.* durazno (may-loh-coh-TOHN; doo-RAHS-noh)

peak n. pico; (PEE-coh)

peanut n. maní; *Mex.* cacahuate (mah-NEE; cah-cah-oo-AH-tay)

pearl n. perla (PAYR-lah)

peasant n. campesino; *Cuba* guajiro; *PR* jíbaro (cahm-pay-SEE-noh; gwah-HEE-roh; HEE-bah-roh)

pedestrian n. peatón (pay-ah-TOHN)

pen n. pluma (PLOO-mah)

pencil n. lápiz (LAH-pees)

penny n. centavo (sayn-TAH-voh)

people n. gente (HAYN-tay)

pepper n. pimienta (pee-mee-AYN-tah)

per prep. por (pohr)

percent n., adj. por ciento (pohr see-AYN-toh)

percentage n. porcentaje (pohr-sayn-TAH-hay)

performance n. función (foon-see-OHN)

perfume n. perfume (payr-FOO-may)

perhaps adv. quizás (key-SAHS)

permission n. permiso (payr-MEE-soh)

permit v. permitir (payr-mee-TEER)

person n. persona (payr-SOH-nah)

petroleum n. petróleo (pay-TROH-lay-oh)

photograph n. foto; v. sacar foto (FOH-toh; sah-CAHR FOH-toh)

picture n. cuadro (KWAH-droh)

pie n. *Arg.* torta; *Cuba* pastel; *Mex.* pay (TOHR-tah; PAHS-tayl; pay)

pillow n. almohada (ahl-moh-AH-dah)

pineapple n. piña; *Arg.* ananá (PEE-nyah; ah-nah-NAH)

pink adj. rosado (roh-SAH-doh)

place n. lugar; v. poner (loo-GAHR; poh-NAYR)

plane n. avión (ah-vee-OHN)

plant n. planta; v. plantar (PLAHN-tah; plahn-TAHR)

plate n. plato (PLAH-toh)

play n. drama; v. jugar (DRAH-mah; hoo-GAHR)

police n. policía; *Arg.* botón (poh-lee-SEE-ah; boh-TOHN)

pool n. piscina; *Mex.* alberca (pee-SEE-nah; ahl-BAYR-cah)

poor adj. pobre (POH-bray)

pop n. refresco; gaseosa (ray-FRAYS-coh; gah-say-OH-sah)

popcorn n. *Bol.* pipocas; *Cuba* rositas de maíz; *Mex.* palomitas (pee-POH-cahs; roh-SEE-tahs day mah-EES; pah-loh-MEE-tahs)

pork n. carne de puerco (CAHR-nay day PWAYR-coh)

port n. puerto (PWAYR-toh)

position n. posición (poh-see-see-OHN)

possible adj. posible (poh-SEE-blay)

postcard n. tarjeta postal (tahr-HAY-tah pohs-TAHL)

post office n. casa de correos; *Mex.* oficina de correos (CAH-sah day coh-RAY-ohs; oh-fee-SEE-nah day coh-RAY-ohs)

potato n. papa (PAH-pah)

pound n. libra (LEE-brah)

power n. poder (poh-DAYR)

practice v. practicar (prak-tee-CAHR)

prefer v. preferir (pray-fay-REER)

prepare v. preparar (pray-pah-RAHR)

prescription n. (med.) receta (ray-SAY-tah)

present v. presentar (pray-sayn-TAHR)

president n. presidente (pray-see-DAYN-tay)

pretty adj. bonito (boh-NEE-toh)

price n. precio (PRAY-see-oh)

priest n. cura (COO-rah)

printer n. impresor (eem-pray-SOHR)

prison n. prisión (pree-see-OHN)

private adj. privado (pree-VAH-doh)

probable adj. probable (proh-BAH-blay)

problem n. problema (proh-BLAY-mah)

produce v. producir (proh-doo-SEER)

product n. producto (proh-DOOK-toh)

prohibit v. prohibir (proh-ee-BEER)

promise v. prometer (proh-may-TAYR)

prostitute n. prostituta (prohs-tee-TOO-tah)

protection n. protección (proh-tayk-see-OHN)

public n., adj. público (POO-blee-coh)

pull v. tirar; jalar (tee-RAHR; hah-LAHR)

punctual adj. puntual (poon-too-AHL)

pure adj. puro (POO-roh)

purple n., adj. morado (moh-RAH-doh)

purpose n. propósito (proh-POH-see-toh)

purse n. bolsa (BOHL-sah)

push v. empujar (aym-poo-HAHR)

put v. poner (poh-NAYR)

put on v. poner(se) (poh-NAYR-say)

pyramid n. pirámide (pee-RAH-mee-day)

Q

quality n. calidad (cah-lee-DAHD)

quantity n. cantidad (cahn-tee-DAHD)

question n. pregunta v. preguntar (pray-GOON-tah; pray-goon-TAHR)

quiet adj. tranquilo (trahn-KEY-loh)

quite adv. bastante (bahs-TAHN-tay)

R

radio n. radio (RAH-dee-oh)

railway n. ferrocarril (fay-roh-cah-REEL)

rain n. lluvia; v. llover (YOO-vee-ah; yoh-VAYR)

raincoat n. impermeable (eem-payr-may-AH-blay)

raise v. levantar (lay-vayn-TAHR)

rapid adj. rápido (RAH-pee-doh)

rare adj. medio crudo (MAY-dee-oh CROO-doh)

rate n. tarifa (tah-REE-fah)

rate of exchange n. tipo de cambio (TEE-poh day CAHM-bee-oh)

razor n. máquina de afeitar (MAH-key-NAH day ah-fay-TAHR)

razor blade n. hoja de afeitar; *Mex.* hoja de rasurar (OH-hah day ah-fay-TAHR; OH-hah day rah-soo-RAHR)

read v. leer (lay-AYR)

ready adj. listo (LEES-toh)

real adj. verdadero (vayr-dah-DAY-roh)

realize v. dar(se) cuenta de (dahr-say coo-AYN-tah day)

receipt n. recibo (ray-SEE-boh)

receive v. recibir (ray-see-VEER)

recent adj. reciente (ray-see-AYN-tay)

recognize v. reconocer (ray-coh-noh-SAYR)

recommend v. recomendar (ray-coh-mayn-DAHR)

red n., adj. rojo (ROH-hoh)

refer v. referir (ray-fay-REER)

refuse v. rehusar (ray-oo-SAHR)

register n. registro (ray-HEES-troh)

rely v. confiar (cohn-fee-AHR)

remain v. quedar(se) (kay-DAHR-say)

remember v. recordar (ray-cohr-DAHR)

remit v. remitir (ray-mee-TEER)

repeat v. repetir (ray-pay-TEER)

reply n. respuesta; v. responder (rays-PWAYS-tah; rays-pohn-DAYR)

report n. informe; v. informar (een-FOHR-may; een-fohr-MAHR)

request v. pedir (pay-DEER)

reservation n. reservación (ray-sayr-vah-see-OHN)

reserve v. reservar (ray-sayr-VAHR)

responsible adj. responsable (rays-pohn-SAH-blay)

rest v. descansar (days-cahn-SAHR)

restaurant n. restaurante (rays-tah-oo-RAHN-tay)

retail n. venta al menudeo (VAYN-tah ahl may-noo-DAY-oh)

return v. regresar; volver (ray-gray-SAHR; vohl-VAYR)

rice n. arroz (ah-ROHS)

rich adj. rico (REE-coh)

right n. derecho; adj. correcto; derecho (direction) (day-RAY-choh; coh-RAYK-toh)

right now adv. ahora mismo; *Ec.*, *Mex.* ahorita (ah-OH-rah MEES-moh; ah-oh-REE-tah)

right there adv. allí mismo (ah-EE MEES-moh)

river n. río (REE-oh)

road n. camino (cah-MEE-noh)

roast n. asado (ah-SAH-doh)

rob v. robar (roh-BAHR)

robber n. ladrón (lah-DROHN)

room n. cuarto; habitación; *Arg.*, *Chi.* pieza (KWAHR-toh; ah-bee-tah-see-OHN; pee-AY-sah)

route n. ruta (ROO-tah)

rubbish n. basura (bah-SOO-rah)

ruby n. rubí (roo-BEE)

rug n. alfombra; *Mex.* tapete (ahl-FOHM-brah; tah-PAY-tay)

rum n. ron (rohn)

run v. correr (coh-RAYR)

rush v. ir de prisa (eer day PREE-sah)

S

sad adj. triste (TREES-tay)

safe n. caja de seguridad; adj. seguro (CAH-hah day say-goo-ree-DAHD; say-GOO-roh)

safety n. seguridad (say-goo-ree-DAHD)

salad n. ensalada (ayn-sah-LAH-dah)

salary n. salario (sah-LAH-ree-oh)

sale n. venta; *Mex.* barata (VAYN-tah; bah-RAH-tah)

salt n. sal (sahl)

same adj. mismo (MEES-moh)

sample n. muestra (moo-AYS-trah)

sandwich n. sandwich; emparedado; *Cuba* bocadito; *Ec.* sánduche (SAHN-doo-eech; aym-pah-ray-DAH-doh; boh-cah-DEE-toh; SAHN-doo-chay)

satisfactory adj. satisfactorio (sah-tees-fahk-TOH-ree-oh)

Saturday n. sábado (SAH-bah-doh)

sauce n. salsa (SAHL-sah)

sausage n. salchicha (frankfurter) (sahl-CHEE-chah)

save v. salvar; ahorrar (money) (sahl-VAHR; ah-oh-RAHR)

say v. decir (day-SEER)

schedule n. horario (oh-RAH-ree-oh)

school n. escuela (ess-KWAY-lah)

scissors n. tijeras (tee-HAY-rahs)

sculptor n. escultor (ays-cool-TOHR)

sea n. mar (mahr)

season n. estación (ess-tah-see-OHN)

seat n. asiento; v. sentar (ah-see-AYN-toh; sayn-TAHR)

secretary n. secretario/a (say-cray-TAH-ree-oh/ah)

security n. seguridad (say-goo-ree-DAHD)

see v. ver (vayr)

seek v. buscar (boos-CAHR)

seem v. parecer (pah-ray-SAYR)

sell v. vender (vayn-DAYR)

send v. enviar (ayn-vee-AHR)

separate adj. separado (say-pah-RAH-doh)

separate v. separar (say-pah-RAHR)

separation n. separacion (say-pah-rah-see-OHN)

September n. septiembre (sayp-tee-AYM-bray)

servant n. criado; sirviente (cree-AH-doh; seer-vee-AYN-tay)

service n. servicio (sayr-VEE-see-oh)

seven n., adj. siete (see-AY-tay)

seventy n., adj. setenta (say-TAYN-tah)

several adj. varios (VAH-ree-ohs)

shampoo n. champú (chahm-POO)

share n. (com.) acción; v. compartir (ahk-see-OHN; cohm-pahr-TEER)

shareholder n. (com.) accionista (ahk-see-ohn-NEES-tah)

shark n. tiburón (tee-BOO-rohn)

sharp adj. agudo (ah-GOO-doh)

shave v. afeitar(se); *CA, Mex.* rasurar(se) (ah-fay-TAHR-say; rah-soo-RAHR-say)

she pron. ella (AY-yah)

sheet n. hoja (paper); sábana (bed) (OH-hah; SAH-bah-nah)

shellfish n. mariscos (mah-REES-cohs)

sherry n. vino de jerez (VEE-noh day hay-RAYS)

shirt n. camisa (cah-MEE-sah)

shoe n. zapato (sah-PAH-toh)

shoeshine boy n. limpiabotas; *Mex.* bolero (leem-pee-ah-BOH-tahs; boh-LAY-roh)

shop n. tienda; v. ir de compras (tee-AYN-dah; eer day COHM-prahs)

short adj. corto; bajo (stature) (COHR-toh; BAH-hoh)

shout v. gritar (gree-TAHR)

show v. mostrar (mohs-TRAHR)

shower n. *Carib.* ducha; *Mex.* regadera (DOO-chah; ray-gah-DAY-rah)

shrimp n. camarones (cah-mah-ROHN-´ys)

sick adj. malo; enfermo (MAH-loh; ayn-FAYR-moh)

sidewalk n. acera; *Arg., CA, Mex.* banqueta (ah-SAY-rah; bahn-KAY-tah)

sign v. firmar (feer-MAHR)

signature n. firma (FEER-mah)

silk n. seda (SAY-dah)

silver n. plata (PLAH-tah)

simple adj. sencillo (sayn-SEE-yoh)

since adv. desde (DAYS-day)

sing v. cantar (cahn-TAHR)

singer n. cantante (cahn-TAHN-tay)

sister n. hermana (ayr-MAH-nah)

sit down v. sentar(se) (sayn-TAHR-say)

six n., adj. seis (says)

sixty n., adj. sesenta (say-SAYN-tah)

size n. tamaño (tah-MAH-nyoh)

skin n. piel (pee-AYL)

skirt n. falda; *Cuba* saya (FAHL-dah; SAH-yah)

sleep n. sueño; v. dormir (SWAY-nyo; dohr-MEER)

sleeve n. manga (MAHN-gah)

slow adj. lento (LAYN-toh)

slowly adv. despacio (days-PAH-see-oh)

small adj. pequeño; chico (pay-KAY-nyoh; CHEE-coh)

smart adj. inteligente (een-tay-lee-HAYN-tay)

smoke v. fumar (foo-MAHR)

snack n. merienda; *Chi.* las onces; *Mex.* botanas (may-ree-AYN-dah; lahs OHN-says; boh-TAH-nahs)

soap n. jabón (hah-BOHN)

soccer n. fútbol; balompié (FOOT-bohl; bah-lohm-pee-AY)

society n. sociedad (soh-see-ay-DAHD)

sock n. calcetín; media (cahl-say-TEEN; MAY-dee-ah)

soft drink n. refresco; *Pe.* gaseosa (ray-FRAYS-coh; gah-say-OH-sah)

sole n. suela (shoe) (SWAY-lah)

solve v. resolver (ray-sohl-VAYR)

some adj. algunos; unos (ahl-GOO-nohs; OO-nohs)

somebody n., pron. alguien (AHL-ghee-ayn)

something n., pron. algo (AHL-goh)

sometimes adv. a veces (ah VAY-says)

son n. hijo (EE-hoh)

song n. canción (cahn-see-OHN)

soon adv. pronto (PROHN-toh)

soup n. sopa (SOH-pah)

south n. sur (soor)

souvenir n. recuerdo (ray-KWAYR-doh)

speak v. hablar (ah-BLAHR)

special adj. especial (ess-pay-see-AHL)

speech n. discurso (dees-COOR-soh)

spend v. gastar (gah-STAHR)

spicy adj. picante (pee-CAHN-tay)

spinach n. espinacas (ess-pee-NAH-cahs)

spoon n. cuchara (coo-CHAH-rah)

sport n. deporte (day-POHR-tay)

spring n. primavera (pree-mah-VAYR-ah)

staff n. personal (payr-soh-NAHL)

stairs n. escalera (ess-cah-LAY-rah)

stamp n. estampilla; *Arg.*, *Cuba* sello; *Mex.* timbre (ess-tahm-PEE-yah; SAY-yoh; TEEM-bray)

start v. comenzar; empezar (coh-mayn-SAHR; aym-pay-SAHR)

state n. estado (ess-TAH-doh)

statement n. declaración; (com.) estado de cuenta (day-clah-rah-see-OHN; ess-TAH-doh day coo-AYN-tah)

station n. estación (ess-tah-see-OHN)

stationery store n. papelería (pah-pay-lay-REE-ah)

statue n. estatua (ess-TAH-too-ah)

stay v. quedar(se) (kay-DAHR-say)

steak n. biftec; *RP* bife (beef-TAYK; BEE-fay)

steal v. robar (roh-BAHR)

stew n. *Mex.* guisado *RP* guiso (ghee-SAH-doh; GHEE-soh)

still adv. todavía (toh-dah-VEE-ah)

stockbroker n. corredor de bolsa (coh-ray-DOHR day BOHL-sah)

stock exchange n. bolsa (BOHL-sah)

stockings n. medias (MAY-dee-ahs)

stomach n. estómago (ess-TOH-mah-goh)

stomachache n. dolor de estómago (doh-LOHR day ess-TOH-mah-goh)

stop n. parada; v. detener (pah-RAH-dah; day-tayn-AYR)

store n. tienda (tee-AYN-dah)

straight adj., adv. derecho (day-RAY-choh)

straw (drinking) n. *Bol.* bombilla; *Chi.*, *Uru.* pajita; *Mex.* popote (bohm-BEE-yah; pah-HEE-tah; poh-POH-tay)

strawberry n. fresa (FRAY-sah)

street n. calle (CAH-yay)

strong adj. fuerte (FWAYR-tay)

struggle n. lucha; v. luchar (LOO-chah; loo-CHAHR)

student n. estudiante (ess-too-dee-AHN-tay)

study v. estudiar (ess-too-dee-AHR)

subway n. subterráneo; *Mex.* metro (soob-tay-RAH-nay-oh; MAY-troh)

success n. éxito (EX-ee-toh)

such adj., pron. tal (tahl)

suddenly adv. de repente (de ray-PAYN-tay)

sugar n. azúcar (ah-SOO-cahr)

suit n. traje (TRAH-hay)

summer n. verano (vay-RAH-noh)

sun n. sol (sohl)

Sunday n. domingo (doh-MEEN-goh)

sure adj. seguro (say-GOO-roh)

sweater n. suéter (SWAY-tayr)

sweet adj. dulce (DOOL-say)

swim v. nadar (nah-DAHR)

swimming pool n. piscina; *Mex.* alberca (pee-SEE-nah; ahl-BAYR-cah)

system n. sistema (sees-TAY-mah)

T

table n. mesa (MAY-sah)

tail n. cola (COH-lah)

take v. tomar; llevar (toh-MAHR; yay-VAHR)

take away v. quitar (key-TAHR)

take care of v. cuidar (coo-ee-DAHR)

take off v. quitar(se) (key-TAHR-say)

talk v. hablar (ah-BLAHR)

tall adj. alto (AHL-toh)

tasty adj. sabroso; rico (sah-BROH-soh; REE-coh)

tax n. impuesto (eem-PWAYS-toh)

taxi n. taxi; *Arg.* tacho; *Cuba* máquina (TAHK-see; TAH-choh; MAH-key-nah)

tea n. té (tay)

teach v. enseñar (ayn-say-NYAHR)

team n. equipo (ay-KEY-poh)

technical adj. técnico (TAYK-nee-coh)

telegram n. telegrama (tay-lay-GRAH-mah)

telephone n. teléfono; v. llamar por teléfono (tay-LAY-foh-noh; yah-MAHR pohr tay-LAY-foh-noh)

telephone directory n. guía; *Mex.* directorio telefónico (GHEE-ah; dee-rayk-TOH-ree-oh tay-lay-FOH-nee-coh)

temperature n. temperatura; (med.) fiebre; *Mex.* calentura (taym-pay-rah-TOO-rah; fee-AY-bray; cah-layn-TOO-rah)

ten n., adj. diez (dee-AYS)

tennis n. tenis (TAY-nees)

tent n. tienda de campaña (tee-AYN-dah day cahm-PAH-nyah)

terrible adj. terrible (tay-REE-blay)

than conj. que (kay)

Thank you. Gracias. (GRAH-see-ahs)

That's it! ¡Eso es! (ESS-oh ays)

the art. el, la, los, las (el; lah; lohs; lahs)

theater n. teatro (tay-AH-troh)

their adj. su (soo)

then adv. entonces (ayn-TOHN-says)

there adv. allí (ah-EE)

they pron. ellos (AY-yohs)

thief n. ladrón (lah-DROHN)

thin adj. delgado (dayl-GAH-doh)

thing n. cosa (COH-sah)

think v. pensar (payn-SAHR)

thirteen n., adj. trece (TRAY-say)

thirty n., adj. treinta (TRAYN-tah)

thousand n., adj. mil (meel)

three n., adj. tres (trays)

throat n. garganta (gahr-GHAN-tah)

Thursday n. jueves (hoo-WAY-vays)

ticket n. boleto; *Bol.* entrada (boh-LAY-toh; ayn-TRAH-dah)

tie n. corbata (cohr-BAH-tah)

tile n. azulejo (ah-SOO-lay-hoh)

till prep. hasta; conj. hasta que (AH-stah kay)

time n. tiempo; hora (of day) (tee-AYM-poh; OH-rah)

tip n. propina (proh-PEE-nah)

tire n. llanta; *Chi.*, *Uru.* neumático; *Cuba* goma (YAHN-tah; nay-oo-MAH-tee-coh; GOH-mah)

tired adj. cansado (cahn-SAH-doh)

to prep. a (ah)

tobacco n. tabaco (tah-BAH-coh)

today adv. hoy (oy)

toe n. dedo del pie (DAY-doh dayl pee-AY)

toilet n. inodoro (een-oh-DOH-roh)

toll n. tarifa (tah-REE-fah)

tomato n. tomate; *Mex.* jitomate (toh-MAH-tay; hee-toh-MAH-tay)

tomorrow adv. mañana (mah-NYAH-nah)

tonight n., adv. esta noche (ESS-tah NOH-chay)

too adv. también (tahm-bee-AYN)

too much adv. demasiado (day-mah-see-AH-doh)

tooth n. diente; muela (dee-AYN-tay; moo-AY-lah)

toothache n. dolor de muela (doh-LOHR day moo-AY-lah)

towel n. toalla (toh-AH-yah)

town n. pueblo (PWAY-bloh)

traffic n. tráfico (TRAH-fee-coh)

train n. tren (trayn)

translate v. traducir (trah-doo-CEER)

translation n. traducción (trah-dook-see-OHN)

travel v. viajar (vee-ah-HAHR)

trip n. viaje (vee-AH-hay)

truck n. camión (cah-mee-OHN)

true adj. verdadero (vayr-dah-DAY-roh)

trunk n. baúl (chest) (bah-OOL)

try v. probar; intentar (proh-BAHR; een-tayn-TAHR)

try on v. probar(se) (proh-BAHR-say)

Tuesday n. martes (MAHR-tays)

turn off v. apagar (ah-pah-GAHR)

turn on v. encender (ayn-sayn-DAYR)

twelve n., adj. doce (DOH-say)

twenty n., adj. veinte (VAYN-tay)

two n., adj. dos (dohs)

typical adj. típico (TEE-pee-coh)

U

ugly adj. feo (FAY-oh)

umbrella n. paraguas (pah-RAH-gwahs)

uncomfortable adj. incómodo (een-COH-moh-doh)

under prep. debajo de (day-BAH-hoh day)

underneath adv. debajo (day-BAH-hoh)

understand v. comprender (cohm-prayn-DAYR)

understanding n. entendimiento (ayn-tayn-dee-mee-AYN-toh)

underwear n. ropa interior (ROH-pah een-tay-ree-OHR)

union n. sindicato (trade) (seen-dee-CAH-toh)

university n. universidad (oo-nee-vahr-see-DAHD)

unless conj. a menos (de) que (ah MAY-nohs day kay)

unmarried adj. soltero (sohl-TAY-roh)

unoccupied adj. desocupado (days-oh-coo-PAH-doh)

unpleasant adj. desagradable (days-ah-grah-DAH-blay)

until prep. hasta; conj. hasta que (AH-stah kay)

up adv. arriba (ah-REE-bah)

upon prep. sobre (SOH-bray)

urban adj. urbano (oor-BAH-noh)

urgent adj. urgente (oor-HAYN-tay)

us pron. nos; nosotros (nohs; noh-SOH-trohs)

use n. uso (OO-soh)

use v. usar (oo-SAHR)

useful adj. útil (OO-teel)

usual adj. usual (oo-soo-AHL)

V

vacancy n. vacancia (vah-CAHN-see-ah)

valid adj. válido (VAH-lee-doh)

valley n. valle (VAH-yay)

valuable adj. valioso (vah-lee-OH-soh)

valuables n. objetos de valor (ohb-HAY-tohs day vah-LOHR)

value n. valor (vah-LOHR)

vanilla n. vainilla (vah-ee-NEE-yah)

various adj. varios (VAH-ree-ohs)

veal n. ternera (tayr-NAY-rah)

vegetable n., adj. vegetal (vay-hay-TAHL)

vendor v. vendedor (vayn-day-DOHR)

very adv. muy (MOO-ee)

view n. vista (VEE-stah)

visa n. visa (VEE-sah)

visit v. visitar (vee-see-TAHR)

visitor n. visitante (vee-see-TAHN-tay)

voice n. voz (vohs)

vomit v. vomitar (voh-mee-TAHR)

W

wages n. sueldo (SWAYL-doh)

wait v. esperar (ess-pay-RAHR)

waiter n. mozo; *Cuba* camarero; *Mex.* mesero (MOH-soh; cah-mah-RAY-roh; may-SAY-roh)

wait for v. esperar (ess-pay-RAHR)

waitress n. *Cuba* camarera; *Mex.* mesera (cah-mah-RAY-rah; may-SAY-rah)

walk v. caminar (cah-mee-NAHR)

wall n. pared (pah-RAYD)

wallet n. billetera (bee-yay-TAY-rah)

want v. desear; querer (day-say-AHR; kay-RAYR)

warehouse n. almacén; bodega (ahl-may-SAYN; boh-DAY-gah)

warm adj. caliente (cah-lee-AYN-tay)

wash v. lavar(se) (lah-VAHR-say)

watch n. reloj; v. mirar (ray-LOH; mee-RAHR)

water n. agua (AH-gwah)

we pron. nosotros (noh-SOH-trohs)

weak adj. débil (DAY-beel)

weapon n. arma (AHR-mah)

wear v. llevar (yay-VAHR)

weary adj. cansado (cahn-SAH-doh)

weather n. tiempo (tee-AYM-poh)

Wednesday n. miércoles (mee-AYR-coh-lays)

week n. semana (say-MAH-nah)

weekday n. día laborable (DEE-ah lah-bohr-AH-blay)

weekend n. fin de semana (feen day say-MAH-nah)

weight n. peso (PAY-soh)

welcome adj. bienvenido (bee-ayn-vay-NEE-doh)

well adj., adv. bien (bee-AYN)

well done adj. bien cocido (bee-AYN coh-SEE-doh)

west n. oeste (oh-AY-stay)

what interr. ¿qué?; pron. lo que (kay; loh kay)

whatever adj. cualquier; pron. cualquiera (kwal-key-AYR; kwal-key-AY-rah)

wheel n. rueda (roo-AY-dah)

when adv. cuando; interr. ¿cuándo? (KWAN-doh)

where adv. donde; conj. donde; interr. ¿dónde? (DOHN-day)

whether conj. si (see)

while conj. mientras que (mee-AYN-trahs kay)

whisky n. whisky

white n., adj. blanco (BLAHN-coh)

who pron. quien; el que; interr. ¿quién? (key-AYN; el kay)

whole adj. entero (ayn-TAY-roh)

wholesale adj., adv. al por major (ahl pohr mah-YOHR)

why interr. ¿por qué? (pohr kay)

wide adj. ancho (AHN-choh)

width n. ancho (AHN-choh)

wife n. esposa (ess-POH-sah)

win v. ganar (gah-NAHR)

wind n. viento; aire (vee-AYN-toh; AY-ray)

window n. ventana (vayn-TAH-nah)

wine n. vino (VEE-noh)

wineglass n. copa (COH-pah)

winter n. invierno (een-vee-AYR-noh)

wish v. desear; querer (day-say-AHR; kay-RAYR)

witchcraft n. brujería (broo-hay-REE-ah)

with prep. con (cohn)

without prep. sin (seen)

woman n. mujer (moo-HAYR)

wood n. madera (mah-DAY-rah)

wool n. lana (LAH-nah)

word n. palabra (pah-LAH-brah)

work n. trabajo; v. trabajar (trah-BAH-hoh; trah-bah-HAHR)

world n. mundo (MOON-doh)

worry v. preocupar(se) (pray-oh-coo-PAHR-say)

worse adj., adv. peor (pay-OHR)

write v. escribir (ess-cree-VEER)

writer n. escritor (ess-cree-TOHR)

wrong adj. equivocado (ay-key-voh-CAH-doh)

X

X-ray n. rayos X (RAH-yohs AYK-ees)

xylophone n. xilófono (see-LOH-foh-noh)

Y

yacht n. yate (YAH-tay)

year n. año (AHN-yoh)

yearly adj. anual (ah-noo-AHL)

yellow n., adj. amarillo (ah-mah-REE-yoh)

yes adv. sí (see)

yesterday adv. ayer (ay-YAYR)

yet adv. aún; todavía; conj. sin embargo (ah-OON; toh-dah-VEE-ah; seen aym-BAHR-goh)

you pron. tú; usted; ustedes (too; oo-STAY; oo-STAY-days)

young adj. joven (HOH-vayn)

youngster n. joven (HOH-vayn)

your adj. su; tu (soo; too)

Z

zero n. cero (SAY-roh)

zipper n. *CA*, *Cuba* zipper; *Mex.*, *Uru.* cierre (SEE-payr; see-AY-ray)

zone n. zona (SOH-nah)

zoo n. zoológico (soh-LOH-hee-coh)

SPANISH PHRASEBOOK

Common Words and Phrases

Yes.
> Sí
> (see)

No.
> No
> (no)

Please.
> Por favor
> (pohr fah-VOHR)

Excuse me.
> Perdone.
> (payr-DOH-nay)

With your permission.
> Con su permiso.
> (cohn soo payr-MEE-soh)

I don't understand.
> No entiendo.
> (no ayn-tee-AYN-doh)

Please repeat.
> Repita, por favor.
> (Ray-PEE-tah, pohr fah-VOHR)

Slower please.
> Más despacio, por favor.
> (Mahs days-PAH-see-oh, pohr fah-VOHR)

It doesn't matter.
> No importa.
> (No eem-POHR-tah)

No problem.
> No hay problema.
> (No AH-ee proh-BLAY-mah)

COMMON WORDS/PHRASES

I think so.
> Creo que sí.
> (CRAY-oh kay see)

I don't think so.
> Creo que no.
> (CRAY-oh kay no)

I don't know.
> No sé.
> (No say)

More or less
> Más o menos.
> (Mahs oh MAY-nohs)

What's happening?
> ¿Qué pasa?
> (Kay PAH-sah)

Sure, you bet!
> Sí, como no.
> (See, COH-moh no)

How do you say...?
> ¿Cómo se dice...
> (COH-moh say DEE-say...)

Let's go.
> Vámonos.
> (BAH-moh-nohs)

Greetings, Polite Expressions and Small Talk

Good morning.
> Buenos días.
> (BWAY-nohs DEE-ahs)

Good afternoon.
> Buenas tardes.
> (BWAY-nahs TAHR-days)

Good evening, good night.
> Buenas noches.
> (BWAY-nahs NOH-chays)

Hi! Hello!
> ¡Hola!
> (OH-lah)

What's new?
> ¿Qué hay de nuevo?
> (Kay AH-ee day NWAY-voh)

Nothing.
> Nada.
> (NAH-dah)

My name is...
> Me llamo...
> (May YAH-moh...)

What's your name?
> ¿Cómo se llama usted?
> (¿COH-moh say YAH-mah oo-STAY?)

I'd like to introduce you to...
> Quiero presentarle a ...
> (Key-AY-roh pray-sayn-TAHR-lay ah...)

Pleased to meet you.
> Mucho gusto.
> (MOO-choh GOOS-toh)

The pleasure is mine.
> El gusto es mío.
> (El GOOS-toh ess MEE-oh)

How are you?
    ¿Cómo está usted?
    (¿COH-moh ess-TAH oo-STAY?)
How's it going?
    ¿Qué tal?
    (¿Kay tahl?)
Fine, thanks.
    Bien, gracias.
    (Bee-AYN, GRAH-see-ahs)
And you?
    ¿Y usted?
    (¿Ee oo-STAY?)
So-so.
    Así, así.
    (ah-SEE, ah-SEE)
What's the weather like?
    ¿Qué tiempo hace?
    (¿Kay tee-AYM-poh AH-say?)
The weather's fine.
    Hace buen tiempo.
    (AH-say bwayn tee-AYM-poh)
The weather's bad.
    Hace mal tiempo.
    (AH-say mahl tee-AYM-poh)
It's hot.
    Hace calor.
    (AH-say cah-LOHR.)
It's cold.
    Hace frío.
    (AH-say FREE-oh.)
I'm hot.
    Tengo calor.
    (TAYN-goh cah-LOHR.)
I'm cold.
    Tengo frío.
    (TAYN-goh FREE-oh.)

Thanks.

    Gracias.

    (GRAH-see-ahs.)

Thanks a lot.

    Muchas gracias.

    (MOO-chahs GRAH-see-ahs.)

You're welcome.

    De nada/Por nada.

    (Day NAH-dah/Pohr NAH-dah.)

Good-bye.

    Adiós.

    (Ah-dee-OHS.)

Ciao.

    Chao.

    (CHAH-oh.)

Come in.

    Pase.

    (PAY-say.)

What?

    ¿Qué?

    (¿Kay?)

    Mex. ¿Mande?

    (¿MAHN-day?)

Cheers!

    ¡Salud!

    (¡Sah-LOOD!)

Names and Titles

First name
  Nombre
  (NOHM-bray)
Last name
  Apellido
  (ah-pay-YEE-doh)

Sir
  Señor
  (Say-NYOHR)
Madam
  Señora
  (Say-NYOH-rah)
Miss
  Señorita
  (Say-nyoh-REE-tah)
Doctor
  Doctor
  (Dohk-TOHR)
Lawyer
  Licenciado
  (Lee-sayn-see-AH-doh)

Numbers

The cardinal numbers are as follows:

zero
    cero
    (SAY-roh)

one
    uno
    (OO-noh)

two
    dos
    (dohs)

three
    tres
    (trays)

four
    cuatro
    (coo-AH-troh)

five
    cinco
    (SEEN-coh)

six
    seis
    (SAY-ees)

seven
    siete
    (see-AY-tay)

eight
    ocho
    (OH-choh)

nine
    nueve
    (noo-AY-vay)

ten
    diez
    (dee-ESS)
eleven
    once
    (OHN-say)
twelve
    doce
    (DOH-say)
thirteen
    trece
    (TRAY-say)
fourteen
    catorce
    (cah-TOHR-say)
fifteen
    quince
    (KEEN-say)

sixteen
    diez y seis
    (dee-ESS ee SAY-ees)

seventeen
    diez y siete
    (dee-ESS ee see-AY-tay)
eighteen
    diez y ocho
    (dee-ESS ee OH-choh)
nineteen
    diez y nueve
    (dee-ESS ee noo-AY-vay)
twenty
    veinte
    (VAY-een-tay)

After twenty, just add the word *y* (and) plus the digit. Twenty one is "twenty and one," *veinte y uno* (VAY-een-tay ee OO-noh); twenty-two is twenty and two, *veinte y dos* (VAY-ee-tay ee dohs) and so on. Form the numbers from the twenties through the nineties in the same way. For example, forty-nine is "forty and nine," *cuarenta y nueve* (kwah-RAYN-tah ee noo-AY-vay).

The ten-words are as follows:

thirty
> treinta
> (TRAY-een-tah)

forty
> cuarenta
> (kwah-RAYN-tah)

fifty
> cincuenta
> (seen-KWEN-tah)

sixty
> sesenta
> (say-SAYN-tah)

seventy
> setenta
> (say-TAYN-tah)

eighty
> ochenta
> (oh-CHAYN-tah)

ninety
> noventa
> (noh-VAYN-tah)

One hundred, by itself, is *cien* (see-AYN). When the word "hundred" is followed by other numbers it is *ciento* (see-AYN-toh), as in "one hundred one" (*ciento uno*). After 120, the pattern is "one hundred twenty and one," "one hundred twenty and two," and so on. The little word *y* (ee), "and," only goes between the tens and the digits, not between the hundreds and the tens. The pattern is the same throughout the hundreds, which are as follows:

one hundred
    cien
    (see-AYN)
one hundred one
    ciento uno
    (see-AYN-toh OO-noh)
two hundred
    doscientos
    (dohs-see-AYN-tohs)
three hundred
    trescientos
    (trays-see-AYN-tohs)
four hundred
    cuatrocientos
    (kwah-troh-see-AYN-tohs)
five hundred
    quinientos
    (key-nee-AYN-tohs)
six hundred
    seiscientos
    (SAY-ees-see-AYN-tohs)
seven hundred
    setecientos
    (say-tay-see-AYN-tohs)
eight hundred
    ochocientos
    (oh-choh-see-AYN-tohs)

nine hundred
noveciencios

noveciencios
(noh-vay-see-AYN-tohs)

One thousand is simply *mil* (meel). A hundred thousand is *cien mil* (see-AYN meel). A million is *un millón*. It's always used with the preposition *de* before a noun.

Days of the Week

Monday
    lunes
    (LOO-nays)
Tuesday
    martes
    (MAHR-tays)
Wednesday
    miércoles
    (mee-AYR-coh-lays)
Thursday
    jueves
    (hoo-AY-vays)
Friday
    viernes
    (vee-AYR-nays)
Saturday
    sábado
    (SAH-bah-doh)
Sunday
    domingo
    (doh-MEEN-goh)

Months of the Year

January
    enero
    (ay-NAY-roh)
February
    febrero
    (fay-BRAY-roh)
March
    marzo
    (MAHR-soh)
April
    abril
    (ah-BREEL)
May
    mayo
    (MAH-yoh)
June
    junio
    (HOO-nee-oh)
July
    julio
    (HOO-lee-oh)
August
    agosto
    (ah-GOHS-toh)
September
    septiembre
    (sayp-tee-AYM-bray)
October
    octubre
    (ohk-TOO-bray)
November
    noviembre
    (noh-vee-AYM-bray)

December
    diciembre
    (dee-see-AYM-bray)

To form a date such as "Tuesday, November 13, 1999," begin with "Tuesday" (*martes*) followed by "13" (*trece*), the proposition *de,* then "November" (*noviembre*), again the proposition *de* and finally 1999, which is always said in Spanish the same way you say any number, one thousand nine hundred ninety nine. The whole date will be: *martes, trece de noviembre de mil novecientos noventa y nueve.*

Only for the first day of every month do you use the ordinal rather than the cardinal number. For example, the first of December is *el primero de diciembre*. Every day thereafter is expressed with a cardinal number. For example, *el diez de diciembre* is the 10th of December.

Time Expressions

What time is it?
    ¿Qué hora es?
    (¿Kay OH-rah ess?)
    Mex. ¿Qué horas son?
    (¿Kay OH-rahs sohn?)
It's one o'clock.
    Es la una.
    (Ess lah OO-nah.)
It's two o'clock.
    Son las dos.
    (Sohn lahs dohs.)
seconds
    segundos
    (say-GOON-dohs)
minutes
    minutos
    (mee-NOO-tohs)
hours
    horas
    (OH-rahs)
morning
    mañana
    (mah-NYAH-nah)
afternoon
    tarde
    (TAHR-day)
evening, night
    noche
    (NOH-chay)
At what time?
    ¿A qué hora?
    (¿Ah kay OH-rah?)

TIME EXPRESSIONS

on time
    a tiempo
    (ah tee-AYM-poh)
yesterday
    ayer
    (ah-YAYR)
today
    hoy
    (oy)
tomorrow
    mañana
    (mah-NYAH-nah)
always
    siempre
    (see-AYM-pray)
never
    nunca
    (NOON-cah)
day
    día
    (DEE-ah)
month
    mes
    (mays)
year
    año
    (AH-nyoh)

Age

How old are you?

¿Cuántos años tiene?

(¿KWAN-tohs AH-nyohs tee-AY-nay?)

I'm _____ years old.

Tengo _____ años.

(TAYN-goh _____ AH-nyohs.)

THE METRIC SYSTEM

The Metric System

As all of Latin America is on the metric system of weights and measurements, you'll need to know a few equivalents. Here are some of the basic ones:

1 kilo	=	2.2 pounds
1 liter	=	1.1 quarts
3.785 liters	=	1 gallon
0 Centigrade (freezing)	=	32 Fahrenheit
37 Centrigrade	=	98.6 Fahrenheit (body temperature)
1 centimeter	=	.39 inches
2.54 centimeter	=	1 inch
1 kilometer	=	0.62 miles

LODGING

Accommodations in Latin America range from five star luxury hotels to very modest, sometimes quite primitive inns or boardinghouses known variously as *pensiones, hospedajes* (payn-see-OHN-nays, ohs-pay-DAH-hays) or *casas de huéspedes* (CAH-sahs day WAYS-pay-days)..

Communication will be no problem in the luxury hotels as they all have English-speaking staff, as is the case in luxury hotels the world over. It's when you choose to stay in more modest hotels or inns that you will need to know a certain number of key phrases in Spanish. You'll find the following phrases useful:

Do you have a single room?
    ¿Tiene una habitación sencilla?
    (¿Tee-AY-nah OO-mah ah-bee-tah-see-OHN
    sayn-SEE-yah?)
Do you have a double room?
    ¿Tiene una habitación doble?
    (¿Tee-AY-nah oo-nah ah-bee-tah-see-OHN
    DOH-blay?)
Is there a phone in the room?
    ¿Hay teléfono en la habitación?
    (¿AH-ee tay-LAY-foh-noh ayn lah ah-bee-tah-
    see-OHN?)
Is it air conditioned?
    ¿Hay aire acondicionado?
    (¿AH-ee AY-ray ah-cohn-dee-see-oh-NAH-
    doh?)
Does it have a TV set?
    ¿Hay televisión?
    (¿AH-ee tay-lay-vee-see-OHN?)

What's the daily rate?

    ¿Cuánto es por día?

    (¿KWAN-toh ess pohr DEE-ah?)

When's check-out time?

    ¿Cuál es la hora de salida?

    (¿KWAL ess lah OH-rah day sah-LEE-dah?)

Do you accept credit cards?

    ¿Aceptan tarjetas de crédito?

    (¿Ah-SAYP-tahn tahr-HAY-tahs day CRAY-dee-toh?)

Questions you'll want to be sure to ask when you consider staying in the more rustic establishments include the following:

Is there always water?

    ¿Siempre hay agua?

    (¿See-AYM-pray AH-ee AH-gwah?)

Is there always hot water?

    ¿Siempre hay agua caliente?

    (¿See-AYM-pray AH-ee AH-gwah cah-lee-AYN-tay?)

Will our luggage be safe?

    ¿Va a estar seguro nuestro equipaje?

    (¿Bah ah ess-TAHR say-GOO-roh noo-AYS-troh ay-key-PAH-hay?)

Is there safe parking? (If driving.)

    ¿Hay estacionamiento seguro?

    (¿AH-ee ess-tah-see-oh-nah-mee-AYN-toh say-GOO-roh?)

I need more water.

    Necesito más agua.

    (Nay-say-SEE-toh mahs AH-gwah.)

...toilet paper.

    ...más papel de baño.

    (...mahs pah-PAYL day BAH-nyoh)

...hangers.
>...más colgadores
>(...mahs cohl-gah-DOHR-ays)
>*Mex.* ...más ganchos
>(...mahs GAHN-chohs.)
>
>*Cuba.* ... más percheros
>(...mahs payr-CHAY-rohs)

To report the breakdown of a fixture or appliance:

The lamp...
>La lámpara...
>(Lah LAHM-pah-rah...)

The toilet...
>El inodoro...
>(El ee-noh-DOH-roh...)

The telephone...
>El teléfono...
>(El tay-LAY-foh-noh...)

The air conditioning...
>El aire acondicionado...
>(El AY-ray ah-cohn-dee-see-oh-NAH-doh...)
>
>*Mex.* El clima...
>(El CLEE-mah...)

The TV...
>El televisor
>(El tay-lay-vee-SOHR...)

...doesn't work.
>...no funciona.
>(...no foon-see-OH-nah.)

At check-out time:

I'd like the bill, please.

> Me dé la cuenta, por favor.
>
> (May day lah KWEN-tah, pohr fah-VOHR.)

There seems to be a mistake.

> Parece que hay un error.
>
> (Pah-RAY-say kay AH-ee oon ay-ROHR.)

Can someone bring down my luggage?

> ¿Me pueden bajar mi equipaje?
>
> (¿May PWAY-dayn bah-HAR mee ay-key-PAH-hay?)

I need a taxi.

> Necesito un taxi.
>
> (Nay-say-SEE-toh oon TAHK-see.)

Telling the hotel staff "Thanks for everything," *Gracias por todo* (GRAH-see-ahs pohr TOH-doh) would end your stay on a gracious note.

THE CUISINES OF LATIN AMERICA

One of the more pleasurable aspects of visiting the countries of Latin America is sampling their various food specialties. So even though the major cities all have restaurants of every type ranging from U.S. style fast food to vegetarian, it is more interesting to seek out those that serve native dishes.

There are similarities in the cuisines of the various Latin American countries, of course, but there are also many differences. A brief listing of the most popular regional dishes follows.

Mexico

The Latin American cuisine best known in the United States is that of Mexico. However, the dishes that are popular in the U.S. are quite limited. In addition to the tacos, enchiladas and tamales popular in the U.S., Mexico offers many delicious regional favorites not well known north of the border. Here are a few examples.

In the state of Jalisco, *pozole* (poh-SOH-lay), a hominy and pork soup served garnished with tortilla chips, lettuce, onions and hot sauce;

In Puebla, *mole poblano* (MOH-lay poh-BLAH-noh), turkey or chicken in a sauce of bitter chocolate, chilies and spices, sprinkled with sesame seeds;

In the Yucatán, be sure to try the *pollo* (POH-yoh) or *cochinito pibil* (coh-chee-NEE-toh pee-BEEL), a chicken or pork dish in a sauce of sour orange juice, garlic and the spice *achiote*, wrapped in banana leaves and baked in a pit;

When in Veracruz, don't miss trying the *huachinango a la veracruzana* (oo-ah-chee-NAHN-goh ah lah vay-rah-croo-SAH-nah), grilled red snapper in a sauce of onions, chili, olives and capers.

Central America

A staple throughout the region is black beans with white rice, often served with fried bananas. In Nicaragua you might try the *nacatemales* (nah-cah-tay-MAHL-ays), meat tamales with salad on top. The less fainthearted might also sample the *mondongo* (mohn-DOHN-goh), or tripe soup. Popular in Panamá and other countries of the region is *sancocho* (sahn-COH-choh), a chicken or meat stew with vegetables. A favorite dish of El Salvador is the *pupusa* (poo-POO-sah). *Pupusas* are thick fried tortillas stuffed with ground pork.

The Caribbean

In the Spanish-speaking regions of the Caribbean the cuisine draws heavily from Spanish cuisine with the addition of native fruits and vegetables. This influence can be found in the heavy soups, or *potajes* (poh-TAH-hays) of Cuba. It is also the reason why a tortilla in this area is not the Mexican flat, thin corn or flour pancake but rather an omelet as it is in Spain. Not to be missed in Puerto Rico as the *asopao* (ah-soh-PAH-oh), a soupy rice stew with chicken or shellfish and the *pernil* (payr-NEEL), the Puerto Rican-style roast pork.

South America

In South America, you will find the following to be among the best known dishes of the various countries:

Argentina - *Parrillado* (pah-ree-YAH-doh), a mixed grill of steak, organ meat and several kinds of sausage;

Bolivia - *Empanada salteña* (aym-pah-NAH-dah sahl-TAY-nyah), a mixture of ground meat or chicken, olives, raisins, potatoes and hot sauce, baked in dough;

Chile - *Pastel de choclo* (pahs-TAYL day CHOH-cloh), a casserole of corn, ground beef, chicken, raisins, onions and hard boiled eggs;

Colombia - *Bandeja paisa* (bahn-DAY-hah PAH-ee-sah), a combination of beans, rice, fried pork rinds, corn cakes, fried plantains, fried eggs and shredded beef;

Ecuador - *Llapingachos* (yah-peen-GAH-chohs), a tasty mashed potato and cheese dish;

Paraguay - *Sopa paraguaya* (SOH-pah pah-rah-GWAY-yah), a mashed corn soup with cheese, milk, eggs and onions. Good with *chipa*, (CHEE-pah) or cheese cornbread;

Peru - *Lomo saltado* (LOH-moh sahl-TAH-doh), stir-fried sirloin, grilled onions and tomatoes, served with rice or french fries;

Uruguay - *Matambre relleno hervido* (mah-TAHM-bray ray-YAY-noh ayr-VEE-doh), boiled beef stuffed with either vegetables or bread crumb dressing;

Venezuela - *Hallaca* (ah-YAH-cah), a mixture of cornmeal with meat, peppers, raisins, olives, onions and spices wrapped in banana leaves and boiled.

Desserts will include the usual fruit, ice cream and pastries served the world around. However, one delicious item found on most menus in the Spanish-speaking world bears special mention. That's the egg custard, *flan* (flahn). It is usually served with a burnt sugar sauce topping and may also be flavored with coconut, orange and the like.

The above is a mere sampling of the extensive cuisines of Latin America. The more adventuresome you are the more taste treats await you. So *¡Buen provecho!* (bwayn proh-VAY-choh). That's Spanish for "Bon appétit."

IN THE RESTAURANT

Just a few key phrases and a little knowledge of food vocabulary is all you'll need for dining out. For example, a waiter will ask you:

What'll you have?
> ¿Qué va a tomar?
> (¿Kay vah ah toh-MAHR?)

To which you respond:
> (<u>Food item</u>), por favor
> _____, (pohr fah-VOHR)

A simple formula for asking the waiter whether the restaurant has a specific item is to say:

> ¿Hay <u>food item</u>?
> (¿AH-ee _____?)

If you're lacking a utensil, just say:
> Necesito un/a _____
> (Nay-say-SEE-toh oon/OO-nah _____.)

cup
> taza
> (TAH-sah)

fork
> tenedor
> (tay-nay-DOHR)
> *Ec., Pe.* trinche
> (TREEN-chay)

glass
> vaso
> (VAH-soh)

knife
> cuchillo
> (coo-CHEE-yoh)

IN THE RESTAURANT

napkin
    servilleta
    (sayr-vee-YAY-tah)

plate
    plato
    (PLAH-toh)
spoon
    cuchara
    (coo-CHAH-rah)

Non-Alcoholic Beverages

hot chocolate
    chocolate caliente
    (choh-coh-LAH-tay cah-lee-AYN-tay)
coffee
    café
    (cah-FAY)
milk
    leche
    (LAY-chay)
soft drink
    refresco
    (ray-FRAYS-coh)
    gaseosa
    (gah-say-OH-sah)
tea
    té
    (tay)
water
    agua
    (AH-gwah)
juice
    jugo
    (HOO-goh)

Dairy Products

butter
    mantequilla
    (mahn-tay-KEY-yah)
cheese
    queso
    (KAY-soh)
eggs
    huevos
    (WAY-vohs)
    ...fried
    ...fritos
    (...FREE-tohs)
    ...scrambled
    ...revueltos
        (...ray-voo-AYL-tohs)

Condiments

gravy
    salsa
    (SAHL-sah)
ketchup
    salsa catsup
    (SAHL-sah CAHT-soop)
mayonnaise
    mayonesa
    (mah-yoh-NAY-sah)
mustard
    mostaza
    (mohs-TAH-sah)
pepper
    pimienta
    (pee-mee-AYN-tah)
salt
    sal
    (sahl)

IN THE RESTAURANT

Meat and Poultry

beef
    carne de res
    (CAHR-nay day rays)
hamburger
    hamburguesa
    (ahm-boor-GAY-sah)
steak
    biftec
    (beef-TAYK)

    Arg. bife
    (BEE-fay)

lamb
    carnero
    (cahr-NAY-roh)
bacon
    tocino
    (toh-SEE-noh)
pork
    carne de puerco
    (CAHR-nay day poo-AYR-coh)
ham
    jamón
    (hah-MOHN)
veal
    ternera
    (tayr-NAY-rah)
liver
    higado
    (EE-gah-doh)
tongue
    lengua
    (LAYN-gwah)

chicken
    pollo
    (POH-yoh)
duck
    pato
    (PAH-toh)
turkey
    pavo
    (PAH-voh)

Seafood

shrimp
    camarones
    (cah-mah-ROHN-ays)
oyster
    ostiones
    (ohs-tee-OH-nays)
lobster
    langosta
    (lahn-GOHS-tah)
crab
    cangrejo
    (cahn-GRAY-hoh)
clams
    almejas
    (ahl-MAY-hahs)
fish
    pescado
    (pays-CAH-doh)

Vegetables

beans (dry)
    Arg., Bol., Chi., Ec., Uru. porotos
    (poh-ROH-tohs)

Cuba, Mex. frijoles
(free-HOH-lays)

beans (green)
  Bol., Uru. habas
  (AH-bahs)

  Chi. porotos verdes
  (poh-ROH-tohs VAYR-days)

  Mex. ejotes
  (ay-HOH-tays)

  RP chauchas
  (CHAH-oo-chahs)

cabbage
  col
  (cohl)

  Mex. repollo
  (ray-POH-yoh)
carrots
  zanahorias
  (sah-nah-OH-ree-ahs)
corn
  maíz
  (mah-EES)

  Mex. elote
  (ay-LOH-tay)

  SA choclo
  (CHOH-cloh)

cucumber
    pepino
    (pay-PEE-noh)
lettuce
    lechuga
    (lay-CHOO-gah)
mushrooms
    champiñones
    (chahm-pee-NYOH-ess)
onion
    cebolla
    (say-BOH-yah)
potato
    papa
    (PAH-pah)
tomato
    tomate
    (toh-MAH-tay)

    Mex. jitomate
    (hee-toh-MAH-tay)

Fruits and Nuts

almonds
    almendras
    (ahl-MAYN-drahs)
apple
    manzana
    (mahn-SAH-nah)
avocado
    aguacate
    (ah-gwah-CAH-tay)

SA palta
(PAHL-tah)

McDonald's in Santiago de Chile serves a McPalta burger!

banana

plátano
(PLAH-tah-noh)

Pan., PR guineo
(ghee-NAY-oh)

Ven. cambur
(cahm-BOOR)

cantaloupe
melón
(may-LOHN)

grapefruit
toronja
(toh-ROHN-hah)

Arg. pomelo
(poh-MAY-loh)

lime
limón
(lee-MOHN)

peach
melocotón
(may-loh-coh-TOHN)

Mex. durazno
(doo-RAHS-noh)

pineapple
  piña
  (PEE-nyah)
strawberry
  fresa
  (FRAY-sah)

Desserts

cake
  Chi., Ec., Uru. torta
  (TOHR-tah)

  Mex. pastel
  (pahs-TAYL)

  PR bizcocho
  (bees-COH-choh)

ice cream
  helado
  (ay-LAH-doh)

  PR mantecado
  (mahn-tay-CAH-doh)

Pie
  Arg. torta
  (TOHR-tah)

  Cuba pastel
  (pahs-TAYL)

  Mex. pay
  (pie)

custard
>   flan
>   (flahn)

The Restroom

Where's the restroom?
>   ¿Dónde está el baño? (¿DOHN-day ess-TAH el BAHN-yoh?)

After enjoying your meal, you can call for the bill by saying:

The bill, please.
>   La cuenta, por favor
>   (Lah KWAYN-tah, pohr fah-VOHR.)

Then don't forget to leave a tip, or *propina* (proh-PEE-nah).

DRINKS

Alcoholic beverages are sold in all manner of drinking establishments throughout Latin America. The luxury bars and restaurants offer the same drink menus to be found in similar places internationally. So when the waiter asks:

"What'll you have?..."
> ¿Qué van a tomar?...
> (¿Kay vahn ah toh-MAHR?)...

your response might well be one of the following:

A Cuba Libre, please.
> Una Cuba Libre, por favor.
> (OO-nah COO-bah LEE-bray, pohr fah-VOHR.)

A margarita, please.
> Una margarita, por favor.
> (OO-nah mahr-gah-REE-tah, pohr fah-VOHR.)

A beer, please.
> Una cerveza, por favor.
> (OO-nah sayr-VAY-sah, pohr fah-VOHR.)

A pina colada, please.
> Una piña colada, por favor.
> (OO-nah PEE-nyah coh-LAH-dah, pohr fah-VOHR.)

The following is a list of your basic alcoholic beverages in Spanish:

beer
> cerveza
> (sayr-VAY-sah)

DRINKS

brandy
>brandy
>(BRAHN-dee)

cognac
>coñac
>(COHN-yak)

gin
>ginebra
>(hee-NAY-brah)

rum
>ron
>(rohn)

scotch
>whisky escocés
>(WEES-kee ess-coh-SAYS)

vodka
>vodka
>(VOHD-kah)

wine
>vino
>(VEE-noh)

red wine
>vino tinto
>(VEE-noh TEEN-toh)

white wine
>vino blanco
>(VEE-noh BLAHN-coh)

rosé wine
>vino rosado
>(VEE-noh roh-SAH-doh)

Most Latin American countries, of course, have their own drink specialties as well and you will miss out if you don't sample them. Here are some recommendations:

Mexico - Mexican beer is superb. The most popular brands include Bohemia, Carta Blanca, Tecate, Dos Equis and Negro Modelo, the latter a dark beer.

As for the spirits, try the tequila, so popular in the U.S. for making margaritas. It's a liquor distilled from the sap of the agave plant. Another Mexican offering is mezcal, a liquor distilled from a plant of the same name. This is not for the fainthearted. It's the one famous for the worm at the bottom of the bottle.

Central America - Native drink specialties include the Costa Rican *guaro*, an alcoholic drink made from sugar cane, and the Guatemalan *boj*, a drink made from fermented corn.

Peru and Bolivia - Try both the *chicha* and the *pisco*. *Chicha* is a corn-based drink which can be either alcoholic or non-alcoholic. *Pisco* is a clear spirit that is typically served in *pisco* sours.

Chile and Argentina - Both countries produce good wines. Particularly to be recommended are the Chilean wines, Santa Carolina and the Casillero del Diablo.

As to what sort of establishment one imbibes in, just be observant of the mores of the country. Women, for example, are often not welcomed in certain bars, particularly if unaccompanied. Foreign travelers should also be circumspect in the comments they make when drinking in bars. It's all too easy to give offense while under the influence.

But do enjoy and offer your fellow tipplers a friendly toast by saying, "Here's to you," or ¡Salud! (¡Sah-LOOD!)

MONEY

As rates of exchange can fluctuate on a daily basis, it is important that you check on the current rate of exchange in the Latin American countries you expect to visit. This information is available in U.S. banks with international departments.

It's wise to take with you money in various forms, a certain amount in U.S. dollars, some currency of the country you're visiting, traveler's checks and credit cards. That way you are unlikely to be stuck without funds in any sort of establishment.

On arrival, acquaint yourself with the local currency as quickly as possible. It helps to think of a frequently used denomination as "about" $5 US or "about" $20 US, etc. Before spending significant amounts of money, be sure you have first done some comparison shopping.

Phrases you'll most probably need include:

Where is there a bank near here?

¿Dónde hay un banco cerca de aquí?

(¿DOHN-day AH-ee oon BAHN-coh SAYR-cah day ah-KEY?)

Where is there an ATM near here?

Mex. ¿Dónde hay un cajero automático cerca de aquí?

(¿DOHN-day AH-ee oon cah-HAY-roh ah-oo-toh-MAH-tee-coh?)

SA ¿Dónde hay una caja rápida cerca de aquí?

(¿DOHN-day AH-ee OO-nah CAH-hah RAH-pee-dah SAYR-cah day ah-KEY?)

I want to exchange some money.

Quiero cambiar dinero.

(Key AY-roh cahm-bee-AHR dee-NAY-roh.)

I want to cash some traveler's checks.

Quiero cambiar cheques de viajero.

(Key-AY-roh cahm-bee-AHR CHAY-kays day
vee-ah-HAY-roh.)

What is the rate of exchange?

¿Cuál es el tipo de cambio?

(¿KWAL ess el TEE-poh day CAHM-bee-oh?)

How many ... per dollar?

¿Cuántos ... por dólar?

(¿KWAHN-tohs ... pohr DOH-lahr?)

Units of Currency

Argentina	- peso	(PAY-soh)
Bolivia	- boliviano	(bah-lee-vee-AH-noh)
Chile	- peso	(PAY-soh)
Colombia	- peso	(PAY-soh)
Costa Rica	- colón	(coh-LOHN)
Cuba	- peso	(PAY-soh)
Dominican Republic	- peso	(PAY-soh)
Ecuador	- sucre	(SOO-cray)
El Salvador	- colón	(coh-LOHN)
Guatemala	- quetzal	(kayt-SAHL)
Honduras	- lempira	(laym-PEE-rah)
Mexico	- peso	(PAY-soh)
Nicaragua	- córdoba	(COHR-doh-bah)
Panama	- balboa	(bahl-BOH-ah)
Paraguay	- guaraní	(gwah-rah-NEE)
Peru	- nuevo sol	(noo-AY-voh sohl)
Uruguay	- peso	(PAY-soh)
Venezuela	- bolívar	(boh-LEE-vahr)

How much is your commission?

¿Cuánto cargan Uds. de comisión?

(¿KWAN-toh CAHR-gahn oo-STAY-days day
coh-mee-see-OHN?)

Vocabulary you may need:

credit card
tarjeta de crédito
(tahr-HAY-tah day CRAY-dee-toh)

cash
efectivo
(ay-fayk-TEE-voh)

coins
monedas
(moh-NAY-dahs)

cashier
caja
(CAH-hah)

change
cambio
(CAHM-bee-oh)

loose change
suelto
(SWAYL-toh)

Mex. feria
(FAY-ree-ah)

money exchange house
casa de cambio
(CAH-sah day CAHM-bee-oh)

When you leave the country by air, be sure to carry some cash on you to pay the usual airport tax. Many a traveler has arrived at an airport in Latin

America completely broke except for their ticket home, only to find that they are not permitted on the plane without paying this tax.

SHOPPING

Shopping In Latin America is a real treat as the offerings in most of these countries are both unique and varied. A number of countries have one or more items that are particularly popular with visiting shoppers. Here, by country, are some of these items.

Argentina, leather goods and articles of *gaucho* dress
Chile, wine, textiles
Bolivia, alpaca shawls, sweaters and rugs
Costa Rica, semi-precious woods
Dominican Republic, amber and mahogany
Ecuador, antique silver and shrunken heads, or *tzantzas* (imitation)
Guatemala, handwoven Indian textiles
Mexico, silver, ceramics, onyx
Paraguay, lace
Peru, antique silver, alpaca rugs
Puerto Rico, carved wooden religious figures (*santos*)
Uruguay, amethysts, suede jackets
Venezuela, charms made of *cochano* gold, gold *cacique* coins bearing faces of Indian chieftains

Except in established stores with fixed prices, bargaining is called for in most parts of Latin America. It should always be done in a polite, respectful manner.

General Phrases

How much is it?
>¿Cuánto vale?
>(¿KWAN-toh VAH-lay?)

That's too expensive.
>Es demasiado caro.
>(Ess day-mah-see-AH-doh CAH-roh.)

Could you lower the price a bit?
>¿Puede bajar el precio un poco?
>(¿PWAY-day bah-HAHR el PRAY-see-oh oon POH-coh?)

I'll give you _____.
>Le doy _____.
>(Lay doy _____.)

I'll take it.
>Me lo/a llevo.
>(May loh YAY-voh.)

Gifts and Souvenirs

books
>libros
>(LEE-brohs)

ceramics
>cerámica
>(say-RAH-mee-cah)

jewelry
>joyería
>(hoh-yay-REE-ah)

postcards
> tarjetas postales
> (tahr-HAY-tahs pohs-TAHL-ays)

shawl
> manta
> (MAHN-tah)

> *Mex.* rebozo
> (ray-BOH-soh)

craft items
> artesanía
> (ahr-tay-sah-NEE-ah)

toys
> juguetes
> (hoo-GAY-tays)

Jewelry

jewelry store
> joyería
> (hoh-yay-REE-ah)

bracelet
> pulsera
> (pool-SAY-rah)

> *Ven.* brazalete
> (brah-sah-LAY-tay)

earrings
> aretes
> (ah-RAY-tays)

> pendientes (dangling)
> (payn-dee-AYN-tays)

Arg., *Chi.* aros
(AH-rohs)

Nic. chapas
(CHAH-pahs)

Uru. caravanas
(cah-rah-VAHN-ahs)

Ven. zarcillos
(sahr-SEE-yohs)

necklace
  collar
  (coh-YAHR)
ring
  anillo
  (ah-NEE-yoh)

What's it made of?
  ¿De qué material es?
  (¿Day kay mah-tay-ree-AHL ays?)
Is it sterling silver?
  ¿Es de plata esterlina?
  (¿Ays day PLAH-tah ays-tayr-LEE-nah?)
Is it real gold?
  ¿Es de oro genuino?
  (¿Ays de OH-roh hay-noo-EE-noh?)
How many karats is it?
  ¿De cuántos kilates es?
  (¿Day KWAHN-tohs kee-LAH-tays ess?)
What kind of metal/stone is it?
  ¿De qué clase de metal/piedra es?
  (¿Day kay CLAH-sah day may-TAHL/pee-AY-drah ess?)

SHOPPING

amber
  ámbar
  (AHM-bahr)
amethyst
  amatista
  ah-mah-TEES-tah
coral
  coral
  (coh-RAHL)
diamond
  diamante
  (dee-ah-MAHN-tay)
emerald
  esmeralda
  (ays-may-RAHL-dah)
glass
  vidrio
  (VEEH-dree-oh)
gold
  oro
  (OH-roh)
ivory
  marfil
  (mahr-FEEL)
jade
  jade
  (HAY-day)
onyx
  ónix
  (OH-neeks)
pearl
  perla
  (PAYR-lah)
ruby
  rubí
  (roo-BEE)

sapphire
    zafiro
    (sah-FEE-roh)
silver
    plata
    (PLAH-tah)
silver-plated
    plateado
    (plah-tay-AH-doh)
turquoise
    turquesa
    (toor-KAY-sah)

Books and Stationary Supplies

bookstore
    librería
    (lee-bray-REE-ah)
newsstand
    kiosco
    (kee-OHS-koh)
stationary store
    papelería
    (pah-pay-lay-REE-ah)
Do you have any books in English?
    ¿Tiene Ud. libros en inglés?
    (¿Tee-AY-nay oo-STAY LEE-brohs ayn een-
    GLAYS?)
How much is this book?
    ¿Cuánto vale este libro?
    (¿KWAN-toh VAH-lay AYS-tay lee-broh?)
...envelopes?
    sobres?
    (SOH-brays?)
...magazines in English?
    resvistas en inglés?
    (ray-VEES-tahs ayn een-GLAYS?)

...maps?
>mapas?
>(MAH-pahs?)

...notebooks?
>cuadernos?
>(kwah-DAYR-nohs?)

...paper?
>papel?
>(pah-PAYL?)

...ballpoint pens?
>bolígrafos?
>(boh-LEE-grah-fohs?)

...pencils?
>lápices?
>(LAH-pee-says?)

Clothing

Where can I buy a...
>¿Dónde puedo comprar...
>(¿DOHN-day PWAY doh cohm-PRAHR
>oon/OO-nah)

...bathing suit?
>traje de bano?
>(TRAH-hay day BAHN-yoh?)

>*Cuba* trusa
>(TROO-sah)

...belt?
>cinturón?
>(seen-too-ROHN?)

...blouse?
>blusa?
>(BLOO-sah?)

...coat?
>abrigo?

(ah-BREE-goh?)

...dress?
    vestido?
    (vays-TEE-doh?)

...hat?
    sombrero?
    (sohm-BRAY-roh?)

...jacket?
    chaqueta?
    (cah-KAY-tah?)

    Cuba saco
    (SAH-coh)

    Mex. chamarra
    (chah-MAH-rah)

    Pe. casaca
    (cah-SAH-cah)

    RP campera
    (cahm-PAY-rah)

...pants?
    pantalón?
    (pahn-tah-LOHN?)

...raincoat?
    impermeable?
    (eem-payr-may-AH-blay?)

    Pan. capote
    (cah-POH-tay)

...shirt?
    camisa?
    (cah-MEE-sah?)

...slip?

> combinación?
> (cohm-bee-nah-see-OHN?)
>
> *Chi., PR* enagua
> (ayn-AH-gwah)
>
> *Cuba* sayuela
> (sah-yoo-AY-lah)
>
> *Mex.* fondo
> (FOHN-doh)
>
> *Pan.* peticote
> (pay-tee-COH-tay)

...socks?

> calcetines?
> (cahl-say-TEE-nays?)

...stockings?

> medias?
> (MAY-dee-ahs?)

...sweater?

> suéter?
> (SWAY-tayr?)

...underwear?

> ropa interior?
> (ROH-pah een-tay-ree-OHR?)

Can I try it on?

> ¿Puedo probarlo?
> (¿PWAY-doh proh-BAHR-loh?)

Where is the fitting room?

> ¿Dónde está el probador?

(¿DOHN-day ays-TAH el pro-bah-DOHR?)

It fits well.

    Me queda bien.

    (May KAY-dah bee-AYN)

It's too...

    Es demasiado...

    (Ays day-mah-see-AH-doh...)

...big/small

    grande/pequeño, chico

    (GRAHN-day/pay-KAYN-nyoh, CHEE-coh)

...long/short

    largo/corto

    (LAHR-goh/COHR-toh)

...loose/tight

    suelto/apretado

    (SWAYL-toh/ah-pray-TAH-doh)

Do you have it in another color?

    ¿Lo tiene en otro color?

    (¿Loh tee-AYN-ay ayn OH-troh coh-LOHR?)

Do you have anything in...?

    ¿Tiene Ud. algo en ...?

    (¿Tee-AYN-ay oos-STAY AHL-goh ayn...)

colors

    colores

    (coh-LOHR-ays)

red

    rojo

    (ROH-hoh)

pink

    rosado

    (roh-SAH-doh)

purple

    morado

    (moh-RAH-doh)

blue
>   azul
>   (ah-ZOOL)

green
>   verde
>   (VAYR-day)

orange
>   color naranja
>   (coh-LOHR nah-RAHN-hah)

yellow
>   amarillo
>   (ah-mah-REE-yoh)

brown
>   moreno, pardo
>   (moh-RAY-noh, PAHR-doh)

>   *Arg.* beige
>   (as in English)

>   *Mex.* café
>   (cah-FAY)

>   *Pe., Uru., Ven.* marrón
>   (mah-ROHN)

grey
>   gris
>   (grees)

black
>   negro
>   (NAY-groh)

white
>   blanco
>   (BLAHN-coh)

fabric
    tela
    (TAY-lah)
chiffon
    gasa
    (GAH-sah)
corduroy
    pana
    (PAH-nah)
cotton
    algodón
    (ahl-goh-DOHN)
flannel
    franela
    (frah-NAY-lah)
linen
    lino
    (LEE-noh)
nylon
    nilón
    (nee-LOHN)
silk
    seda
    (SAY-dah)
velvet
    terciopelo
    (tayr-see-oh-PAY-loh)
wool
    lana
    (LAHN-ah)

Shoes

shoes
    zapatos
    (sah-PAH-tohs)

SHOPPING

boots
> botas
> (BOH-tahs)

sandals
> sandalias
> (sahn-DAH-lee-ahs)

> *Arg.* osotas
> (oh-SOH-tahs)

> *Mex.* huaraches
> (hwah-RAH-chays)

heels
> tacones
> (tah-COHN-ays)

high/low
> altos/bajos
> (AHL-tohs/BAH-hohs)

Are these made of cloth/suede/leather/ rubber?
> ¿Son estos de...tela/gamuza/piel/goma?
> (¿Sohn AYS-tohs day... TAY-lah/gah-MOO-sah/pee-AYL/GOH-mah?)

They are too big/small/narrow/wide.
> Son demasiado...grandes/pequeños/estrechos/anchos
> (Sohn day-mah-see-AH-doh...GRAHN-days/pay-KAY-nyohs/ays-TRAY-chohs/AHN-chohs)

Camera Shop

The camera store is a place where travelers often have occasion to shop. Here are some expressions you may need:

Please develop this roll of film.

    Revelen este rollo, por favor.

    (Ray-VAY-layn ESS-tay ROH-yoh, pohr fah-
    VOHR.)

When will they be ready?

    ¿Cuándo van a estar listas?

    (¿KWAN-doh vahn ah ess-TAHR LEES-tahs?)

The camera doesn't work.

    No funciona la cámara.

    (No foon-see-OH-nah lah CAH-mah-rah.)

film

    película

    (pay-LEE-coo-lah)

rolls of film

    rollos de película

    (ROH-yohs day pay-LEE-coo-lah)

...for a Polaroid camera

    ...para cámara Polaroid

    (...PAH-rah CAH-mah-rah Polaroid)

batteries

    pilas

    (PEE-lahs)

TRANSPORTATION

Every possible means of transportation known to man is available somewhere in Latin America. In addition to the usual plane, train, bus and car options, you'll find a variety of other—sometimes unusual—forms of transportation. These range from the three-wheeled, open-sided vehicles in Mazatlán, Mexico, known as *pulmonías* or "pneumonias," to the *transbordador*, or ferry, that takes you from central Chile to the edge of Antarctica. The lowly truck is a common form of public transportation in Bolivia.

Travelers generally arrive at their destinations in Latin America by air. As all international airlines have English-speaking personnel, communication with them is no problem. However, you'll next need to pass through customs, or the *aduana* (ah-doo-AH-nah), and there the following phrases may be useful:

I have nothing to declare.

No tengo nada que declarar.

(No TAYN-goh NAH-dah kay day-clah-RAHR.)

This is all for my personal use.

Todo es para mi uso personal.

(TOH-doh ess PAH-rah mee OO-soh payr-soh-NAHL)

Do you want me to open my suitcase?

¿Quiere que abra mi maleta?

(¿Key-AY-ray kay AH-brah mee mah-LAY-tah?)

Taxi

If upon arrival, you need a taxi at an airport, find out from the airline personnel whether there is a controlled-fare taxi service to your hotel. Most of the large airports do have them.

Once in town, you should be able to get general information on cab fares at the place you stay. If you have no knowledge whatsoever of the fare structure for taxis, you run a serious risk of being overcharged. Also you should always agree on the fare with the taxi driver before you get in the cab. Once you're in, it's too late to argue the point.

Here are some helpful phrases in dealing with taxis:

I need a taxi.
>Necesito un taxi.
>(Nay-say-SEE-toh oon TAYK-see.)

This is my suitcase.
>Esta es mi maleta.
>(ESS-tah ess mee mah-LAY-tah.)

I want to go to the Hotel _____.
>Quiero ir al Hotel _____.
>(Kee-AY-roh eer ahl Oh-TAYL _____.)

What's the fare?
>¿Cuánto es la tarifa?
>(¿KWAN-toh ess lah tah-REE-fah?)

The word *taxi* will be understood throughout the Spanish-speaking world, but there are other words for it that are used in specific places. In Argentina, a taxi is often called a *tacho* (TAH-choh), a word that originates from a type of underworld slang known as Lunfardo. Cubans traditionally hail cabs in the street by shouting *¡Máquina!*, the standard word for "machine."

TRANSPORTATION

Bus

There are many types and classes of bus service in Latin America as it is probably the commonest and most popular form of transportation. There are, of course, different names for these bus services from country to country. Here are some of them:

City bus:

    Arg., Bol. colectivo
    (coh-layk-TEE-voh)

    Carib. guagua
    (GWAH-gwah)

    Ec. bus
    (boos)

    Col. buseta
    (boo-SAY-tah)

    Mex. camión
    (cah-mee-OHN)

    Pe., Uru. ómnibus
    (OHM-nee-boos)

To find out where the nearest city bus stop is, ask:

Where's the nearest bus stop?
    ¿Dónde está la parada de (appropriate name of bus) más cercana?
    (¿DOHN-day ess-TAH lah pah-RAH-dah day _____ mahs sayr-CAH-nah?)

When you get on a city bus you'll need to ask:

How much is the fare?
    ¿Cúanto es la tarifa?
    (¿KWAN-toh ess lah tah-REE-fah?)

Then tell the driver:

Let me know when we get to _____.
    Avíseme cuando llegamos a _____.
    (Ah-VEE-say-may KWAN-doh yay-GAH-mohs
    ah _____.)

If you need to move through a crowded bus, always say:

Excuse me.
    Permiso.
    (Payr-MEE-soh)

If you want to get off, just call out:

At the next stop, please.
    En la próxima, por favor.
    (Ayn lah PROKS-ee-mah, pohr fah-VOHR).
Intercity bus:
    Arg. micro
    (MEE-croh)

    Bol. flota
    (FLOH-tah)

    Carib., Mex. autobús
    (ah-oo-toh-BOOZ)

    Ec. bus
    (boos)

Pe., Uru. ómnibus
(OHM-nee-boos)

The words for "bus station" include:

estación de autobuses
(ess-tah-SEE-ohn day ah-oo-toh-BOO-says)

Mex. central de autobuses
(sayn-TRAHL day ah-oo-toh-BOO-says)

SA terminal terrestre
(tayr-mee-NAHL tay-RAYS-tray)

Useful phrases for intercity bus travel include:

I need (number) ticket(s) to (destinations) at (time).

Necesito _____ boleto(s) a _____ a las

_____.

(Nay-say-SEE-toh _____ boh-LAY-toh(s) ah lahs _____.)

Are there round trip tickets from _____ to _____?

¿Hay boletos de viaje redondo de _____ a _____?

(¿AH-ee boh-LAY-tohs day vee-AH-hay ray-DOHN-doh day _____ ah _____?)

How long will the trip take?

¿Cuánto tiempo demora el viaje?

(¿KWAN-toh tee-AYM-poh day-MOH-rah el vee-AH-hay?)

Where can I check my luggage?

¿Dónde puedo chequear mi equipaje?

(¿DOHN-day PWAY doh chay-kay-AHR mee ay-key-PAH-hay?)

Although transportation by bus is more extensive than by train, there may be specific train trips you will want to take. Some of the phrases that will help you at a train station are:

I'd like a timetable.

Quiero un horario de trenes.

(Key-AY-roh oon oh-RAH-ree-oh day TRAYN-ays.)

I want a ticket for (Destination) for (date).

Quiero un boleto para _____ para el día

_____ .

(Key-AY-roh oon boh-LAY-toh PAH-rah

_____ PAH-rah el DEE-ah _____.)

One way.

Solo ida.

(SOH-loh EE-dah)

Round trip.

Viaje redondo.

(Vee-AH-hay ray-DOHN-doh.)

When does the train leave?

¿A qué hora sale el tren?

(¿Ah kay OH-rah SAH-lay el trayn?)

From what platform?

¿De qué andén?

(¿Day kay ahn-DAYN?)

Car

There are car rental agencies in all the major cities and airports of Latin America for those who want the independence of moving around on their own wheels. However, communication in car-related situations can call for a rather extensive amount of vocabulary. To begin with, you'll need to get your bearings. The following phrases should help:

TRANSPORTATION

How do I get to _____?
> ¿Cómo llego a _____?
> (¿COH-moh YAY-goh ah _____?)

How many kilometers to _____?
> ¿Cuántos kilómetros a _____?
> (¿KWAN-tohs kee-LOH-may-trohs ah
> _____?)

I'm lost.
> Estoy perdido.
> (Ess-TOY payr-DEE-doh.)

Which way is north?
> ¿Dónde está el norte?
> (¿DOHN-day ess-TAH el NOHR-tay?)

...south?
> ...el sur?
> (el soohr?)

...east?
> ...el este?
> (el AYS-tay?)

...west?
> ...el oeste?
> (el oh-AYS-tay?)

Is there a gas station near here?
> ¿Hay una gasolinera cerca de aquí?
> (¿AH-ee OO-nah gah-soh-lee-NAY-rah
> SAYR-kah day ah-KEY?)

Where's the next gas station?
> ¿Dónde queda la próxima gasolinera?
> (¿DOHN-day KAY-dah lah PROHK-see-mah
> gah-soh-lee-NAY-rah?)

Phrases that will help you at the gas station include:

Fill it up.
> Llénelo.
> (YAY-nay-loh)

Check the oil.

Revise el aceite.

(Ray-VEE-say el ah-SAY-tay)

Is there a mechanic here?

¿Hay un mecánico aquí?

(¿AH-ee oon may-CAHN-nee-coh ah-KEY?)

Change the tire, please.

Cambie la llanta, por favor.

(CAHM-bee-ay lah YAHN-tah, por fah-VOHR.)

When will it be ready?

¿Cuándo estará listo?

(¿KWAN-doh ess-tah-RAH LEES-toh?)

Here is some additional auto-related vocabulary:

car

coche

(COH-chay)

carro

(CAH-roh)

battery

acumulador

(ah-coo-moo-lah-DOHR)

brake

freno

(FRAY-noh)

carburetor

carburador

(cahr-boo-rah-DOHR)

fan

ventilador

(vayn-tee-lah-DOHR)

generator
  generador
  (hay-nay-rah-DOHR)
lights
  luces
  (LOO-says)
motor
  motor
  (moh-TOHR)
oil
  aceite
  (ah-SAY-tay)
radiator
  radiador
  (rah-dee-ah-DOHR)
starter
  marcha
  (MAHR-chah)
tire
  llanta
  (YAHN-tah)

  Chi., Uru. neumático
  (nay-oo-MAH-tee-coh)

  Cuba goma
  (GOH-mah)

  Ven. caucho
  (CAH-oo-choh)
gas
  gasolina
  (gah-soh-LEE-nah)

  Arg. nafta
  (NAHF-tah)

Chi. bencina
(bayn-SEE-nah)

Walking

One of the very best ways of getting to know a foreign country is to explore it on foot. This will put you in close contact with the people and allow you the time to observe their interactions.

To find your way to your destination, you may need to ask directions. The following phrases should help:

Where is...?
    ¿Dónde está...?
    (¿DOHN-day ess-TAH...?)

(Same as above.)
    ¿Dónde queda...?
    (¿DOHN-day KAY-dah...?)
Where's there...?
    ¿Dónde hay...?
    (¿DOHN-day AH-ee...?)
to the right
    a la derecha
    (ah lah day-RAY-chah)
to the left
    a la izquierda
    (ah lah ees-key-AYR-dah)
straight ahead
    derecho
    (day-RAY-choh)
across from
    frente a
    (FRAYN-tay ah)
around the corner
    a la veulta
    (ah la voo-AYL-tah)

next to
>   junto a
>   (HOON-toh ah)

near
>   cerca de
>   (SAYR-cah day)

far from
>   lejos de
>   (LAY-hohs day)

here
>   aquí
>   (ah-KEY)

there
>   allí
>   (ah-YEE)

In Mexico, that all-important highway sign, "Stop," is *Alto*, (AHL-toh); in South America, it's *Pare* (PAHR-ray).

COMMUNICATIONS

Fax and Internet

Long distance communication between the Latin American countries and the United States and other parts of the world is completely up to date. Fax and E-mail are available in most parts of the area, often even in surprisingly small communities. A recent traveler to Chile reports that she located fax service in Punto Arenas, Chile, the southernmost city of importance in the hemisphere "where the Straits of Magellan lap up on the shore."

The major hotels, of course, have communication centers with the most modern technology for the use of their guests. You'll also find Internet access along the main pedestrian streets of such cities as Buenos Aires, Santiago de Chile and Cusco, Peru.

Internet Cafés exist for the use of the public, but they are so popular that it's often difficult to find a free computer. Sometimes it's easier to find a funky little place where a person will be happy to let you use their computer for a small fee. Costs for these services tend to be nominal. Internet access is usually charged for by the hour; fax by the page. There will normally be a small fee for printing out replies.

Language will not be a serious problem in dealing with these services as much of the vocabulary surrounding modern technology is taken directly from the English. Language purists, of course, decry this practice, but that doesn't prevent it from going on. For example, in Spanish, E-mail is:

correo electrónico

(coh-RAY-oh ay-layk-TROH-nee-coh)

However, people tend to simply use the English expression, E-mail.

Long Distance Telephone

As long distance telephone calls placed from hotels are usually very expensive, many people prefer to use phone cards when calling home. They are widely available throughout Latin America where they sold in shops, at newspaper stands and even hawked in the street in such cities as Santiago de Chile, Buenos Aires and Lima. They are sold in different denominations, just as they are in the U.S., and are quite modest in price. In Spanish, they are called:

tarjetas telefónicas
(tahr-HAY-tahs tay-lay-FOH-nee-cahs)

To use them, you simply slide them into a slot in the pay phones until they're used up. If you leave the country before using up a card, you might want to give it to a local person who has been of service to you, just as a good will gesture.

If you do choose to place long distance calls through your hotel, the following phrases will be helpful:

The international operator.
La operadora internacional.
(Lah oh-pay-rah-DOH-rah een-tayr-nah-see-oh-NAHL)
I'd like to place a long distance call.
Quiero hacer una llamada de larga distancia.
(Key-AY-roh ah-SAYR OO-nah yah-MAH-dah day LAHR-gah dees-TAHN-see-ah.)

Collect.

    Por cobrar.

    (Pohr coh-BRAHR)

I'll pay here.

    Por pagar aquí.

    (Pohr pah-GAHR ah-KEY)

The number is _____

    El número es _____.

    (El NOO-may-roh ess _____.)

_____ calling. (Literally "on the part of")

    Por parte de _____

    (Pohr PAHR-tay day _____.)

Person to person.

    Persona a persona.

    (Payr-SOHN-ah ah payr-SOHN-nah)

Station to station.

    A quien conteste.

    (Ah key-AYN cohn-TAYS-tay)

To place a local call in Spanish, begin as follows:

Is Mr. _____ there?

    ¿Está el señor _____?

    (¿Ess-TAH el say-NYOR _____?)

The reply should be either:

Yes, one moment, please.

    Sí, un momento, por favor.

    (See, oon moh-MAYN-toh, pohr fah-VOHR.)

    or

Speaking,

    Él hable,

    (El AH-blah.)

    or

No, he's not in.

>No, no está.

>(No, no ess-TAH.)

If the person you're trying to reach isn't in, you can say:

May I leave a message?

>¿Puedo dejar un recado?

>(¿PWAY-doh day-HAHR oon ray-CAH-doh?)

Tell him to call (your name) at (your number).

>Dígale que llame a _____ a

>_____.

>(DEE-gah-lay kay YAH-may ah _____ ah

>_____.)

People in the different Spanish-speaking countries have several ways of answering the phone. Equivalents of "hello" that you may hear in the various countries include the following:

>¡Aló!

>(¡Ah-LOH!)

>¡ Bueno!

>(¡BWAY-noh!)

>¡ A ver!

>(¡Ah vayhr!)

>¡ Qué hay!

>(¡Kay AH-ee!)

>¡ Oigo!

>(¡OY-goh!)

¡ Dígame!
(¡DEE-gah-may!)

Postal Service

"Snail" mail from Latin America can be as slow as its namesake, so don't be surprised if you get home before your "wish-you-were-here" tourist postcard does. Urgent communication should certainly go the phone, fax or E-mail route.

Hotels often sell stamps as well as post cards. If your hotel does not, you'll need to find a post office, or *Casa de Correo* (CAH-sah day coh-RAY-oh). Post offices in Mexico are called *Oficinas de Correo* (Oh-fee-SEE-nahs day coh-RAY-oh).

To buy postal items, just say:

I want to buy...
> Quiero comprar...
> (Key-AY-roh cohm-PRAHR...)

...stamps
> ...estampillas
> (...ess-tahm-PEE-yahs)

> ...*Arg.*, *Cuba* sellos
> (...SAY-yohs)

> ...*Mex.* timbres
> (...TEEM-brays)

...for the United States.
> ...para los Estados Unidos.
> (...PAH-rah lohs Ess-TAH-dohs Oo-NEE-dohs.)

I want to buy envelopes.
> Quiero comprar sobres.
> (Key-AY-roh cohm-PRAHR SOH-brays.)

How do I mail a package?

¿Cómo envio un paquete por correo?

(¿COH-moh ayn-VEE-oh oon pah-KAY-tay
pohr coh-RAY-oh?)

When will it arrive?

¿Cuándo llegará?

(¿KWAN-doh yay-gah-RAH?)

air mail

por avión

(pohr ah-vee-OHN)

post card

tarjeta postal

(tahr-HAY-tah pohs-TAHL)

HEALTH

Before taking an extensive trip it's always wise to deal with any health problem you may have. If you're due for a checkup of any kind, this is a good time to do it.

However, if you do have health-related problems when you're in a Spanish-speaking country, you'll find the following phrases and vocabulary useful:

I'm sick.

Estoy enfermo/a

(Ess-TOY ayn-FAHR-moh/mah.)

I need a doctor who speaks English.

Necesito a un médico que hable inglés.

(Nay-say-SEE-toh ah oon MAY-dee-coh kay AH-blay een-GLAYS.)

Can he come to the hotel?

¿Puede venir al hotel?

(¿PWAY-day vayn-EER ahl oh-TAYL?)

Where is his office?

¿Dónde está su consultorio?

(¿DOHN-day ess-TAH soo cohn-sool-TOH-ree-oh?)

I need an ambulance.

Necesito una ambulancia.

(Nay-say-SEE-toh OO-nah ahm-boo-LAHN-see-ah.)

I need to go to a hospital.

Necesito ir a un hospital.

(Nay-say-SEE-toh eer ah oon ohs-pee-TAHL.)

The following list of symptoms and illnesses will help you tell the doctor what your problem is:

indigestion
    indigestión
    (in-dee-hays-tee-OHN)
cold
    resfriado
    (rays-free-AH-doh)
flu
    gripe
    (GREE-pay)

    Mex. gripa,
    (GREE-pah)

cough
    tos
    (tohs)
diarrhea
    diarrea
    (dee-ah-RAY-ah)
fever
    fiebre
    (fee-AY-bray)

    Mex. calentura
    (cah-layn-TOO-rah)

earache
    dolor de oído
    (doh-LOHR day oh-EE-doh)
asthma
    asma
    (AHS-mah)
high blood pressure
    presión alta
    (pray-see-OHN AHL-tah)

low blood pressure
    presión baja
    (pray-see-OHN BAH-hah)
burn
    quemadura
    (kay-mah-DOO-rah)
diabetes
    diabetis
    (dee-ah-BAY-tees)
nausea
    náuseas
    (NAH-oo-say-ahs)
vomiting
    vómito
    (VOH-mee-toh)
constipation
    estreñimiento
    (ess-tray-nyee-mee-AYN-toh)

The expression *me duele...* (may DWAY-lay...)
followed by any of the following parts of the body
means "My _____ hurts."

finger
    dedo
    (DAY-doh)
stomach
    estómago
    (ess-TOH-mah-goh)
chest
    pecho
    (PAY-choh)
head
    cabeza
    (cah-BAY-sah)

foot
>   pie
>   (pee-AY)

neck
>   cuello
>   (KWAY-yoh)

shoulder
>   hombro
>   (OHM-broh)

ear
>   oído
>   (oh-EE-doh)

arm
>   brazo
>   (BRAH-soh)

hand
>   mano
>   (MAH-noh)

back
>   espalda
>   (ess-PAHL-dah)

leg
>   pierna
>   (pee-AYR-nah)

ankle
>   tobillo
>   (toh-BEE-yoh)

In case of a dental emergency, you'll find the following helpful:

I need an appointment as soon as possible.
>   Necesito una cita los más pronto posible.
>   (Nay-say-SEE-toh OO-nah SEE-tah loh mahs PROHN-toh poh-SEE-blay.)

I need a temporary filling.

 Necesito una tapadura provisional.

 (Nay-say-SEE-toh OO-nah tah-pah-DOO-rah
 proh-vee-see-oh-NAHL.)

I need something for the pain.

 Necesito algo para el dolor.

 (Nay-say-SEE-toh AHL-goh PAH-rah el doh-
 LOHR.)

I want gas.

 Quiero gas.

 (Key-AY-roh gahs.)

I want a shot.

 Quiero una inyección

 (Key-AY-roh OO-nah in-yek-see-OHN.)

Pharmacies in the Latin American countries
sell many more pharmaceutical products over the
counter than do pharmacies in the U.S. Pharma-
cists will often recommend products they believe
will relieve your ailment and they do tend to be
very knowledgeable.

The following vocabulary will be helpful at the
drug store:

asprin

 aspirina

 (ahs-pee-REE-nah)

antibiotic

 antibiótico

 (ahn-tee-bee-OH-tee-coh)

antiseptic

 antiséptico

 (ahn-tee-SAYP-tee-coh)

antihistamine

 antihistamínico

 (ahn-tee-ees-tah-MEE-nee-coh)

antacid
    antiácido
    (ahn-tee-AH-see-doh)
cough syrup
    jarabe para la tos
    (hah-RAH-bay PAH-rah lah tohs)
eyewash
    lavado de ojos
    (lah-VAH-doh day OH-hohs)
laxative
    purga
    (POOR-gah)
nose drops
    gotas para la nariz
    (GOH-tahs PAH-rah lah nah-REES)
vitamins
    vitaminas
    (vee-tah-MEE-nahs)

PERSONAL CARE

Beauty Shop

Some time during their stay in Latin America women may want professional care for their hair. In most countries, this type of establishment is called a *salón de belleza* (sah-LOHN day bay-YAY-sah), but in some countries it's known as a *peluquería* (pay-loo-kay-REE-ah).

Phrases and vocabulary that will help you in this area include the following:

Where can I have my hair done?
> ¿Dónde puedo arreglarme el pelo?
> (¿DOHN-day PWAY-do ah-ray-GLAHR-may el PAY-loh?)

I want a shampoo and set.
> Quiero un champú y peinado.
> (Key-AY-roh oon chahm-POO ee pay-NAH-doh.)

I'd like a haircut.
> Quiero un corte de pelo.
> (Key-AH-roh oon COHR-tay day PAY-loh.)

I want a permanent.
> Quiero un permanente.
> (Key-AY-roh oon payr-mah-NAYN-tay.)

dye
> tinte
> (TEEN-tay)

bangs
> *SA* cerquillo
> (sayr-KEY-loh)
>
> *Chi.* chasquilla
> (chahs-KEY-yah)

    Col. capul
    (cah-POOL)

    Mex. fleco
    (FLAY-coh)

    Ven. pollina
    (poh-YEE-nah)

hairspray
    spray
    (spray)
gel
    gel
    (hell)
curls
    rizos
    (REE-sohs)

    Bol. ondulación
    (ohn-doo-lah-SEE-ohn)

    Ec. churos
    (CHOO-rohs)

    Mex. chinos
    (CHEE-nohs)

    Pe. crespos
    (CRAYS-pohs)

    Uru. bucles
    (BOO-clays)

hairpin
    horquilla
    (ohr-KEY-yah)

    Cuba hebilla
    (ay-BEE-yah)

    Ec. invisible
    (een-vee-SEE-blay)

    Ven. gancho
    (GAHN-choh)

dryer
    secador
    (say-kah-DOHR)
manicure
    manicura
    (mah-nee-COO-rah)
nails
    uñas
    (OO-nyahs)
nail polish
    esmalte
    (ess-MAHL-tay)

Barbershop

Men seeking hair care will go to a *barbería* (bahr-bay-REE-ah) or a *peluquería* (pay-loo-kay-REE-ah), both words are used for "barbershop" in the Latin American countries. High-style establishments for men in Mexico are called *estéticas para caballeros* (ess-TAY-tee-cahs PAH-rah cah-bah-YAY-rohs).

Here are some helpful phrases:

I'd like a haircut.

> Quiero un corte de pelo.
>
> (Key-AY-roh oon COHR-tay day PAY-loh.)

And a shampoo, please.

> Y un lavado de cabeza, por favor.
>
> (Ee oon lah-VAH-doh day cah-BAY-sah, pohr fah-VOHR.)

Don't cut it too short.

> No me corte mucho.
>
> (No may COHR-tay MOO-choh).

I'd like a shave.

> Aféiteme.
>
> (Ah-FAY-tay-may.)

> *Mex.* Rasúreme.
>
> (Rah-SOO-ray-may)

Laundry/Dry Cleaner

Many hotels provide laundry and dry cleaning service. However, if they do not, you can always find a laundry, *lavandería* (lah-vahn-day-REE-ah) or a dry cleaner, *tintorería* (teen-toh-ray-REE-ah) nearby. If you prefer to do your own laundry, look for a laundromat, or *lavandería automática* (lah-vahn-day-REE-ah ah-oo-toh-MAH-tee-cah).

Here are the words for some common toiletries, cosmetics and over-the counter drugs you may need for your personal care and grooming:

aspirin

> aspirina
>
> (ahs-pee-REE-nah)

bobby pin

> *Chi.* pinche
>
> (PEEN-chay)

Ec. imperdible
(eem-payr-DEE-blay)

Mex., Uru. pasador
(pah-sah-DOHR)

Pan. gancho
(GAHN-choh)

PR horquilla
(ohr-KEE-yah)

comb
    peine
    (PAY-nay)
condoms
    condones
    (cohn-DOH-nays)
cough drops
    pastillas para la tos
    (pahs-TEE-yahs PAH-rah lah tohs)
curlers
    tubos
    (TOO-bohs)
deodorant
    desodorante
    (days-oh-doh-RAHN-tay)
hair brush
    cepillo para el pelo
    (say-PEE-yoh PAH-rah el PAY-loh)
lipstick
    lápiz labial
    (LAH-pees lah-bee-AHL)

    lápiz para los labios
    (LAH-pees PAH-rah lohs LAH-bee-ohs)

makeup
maquillaje
(mah-kee-YAH-hay)

Cuba base
(BAH-say)

mascara
rímel
(REE-mayl)

razor
máquina de afeitar
(MAH-kee-nah day ah-fay-TAHR)

Mex. maquina de rasurar
(MAH-kee-nah day rah-soo-RAHR)

razor blades
hojas de afeitar
(OH-hahs day ah-fay-TAHR)

Arg., *Ec.* gilletes
(gee-LAY-tays)

Cuba cuchillitos de afeitar
(coo-chee-YEE-tohs day ah-fay-TAHR)

Mex. hojas de rasurar
(OH-hahs day rah-soo-RAHR)

sanitary napkins
toallas sanitarias
(toh-AH-yahs sah-nee-TAH-ree-ahs)

shampoo
champú
(chahm-POO)

soap
    jabón
    (hah-BOHN)
suntan lotion
    bronceador
    (brohn-say-ah-DOHR)
toilet paper
    papel higiénico
    (pah-PAYL ee-hee-AYN-nee-coh)
toothbrush
    cepillo para los dientes
    (say-PEE-yoh PAH-rah lohs dee-AYN-tays)
toothpaste
    pasta dental
    (PAHS-tah dayn-TAHL)

ENTERTAINMENT

Sightseeing

Certainly the very first form of entertainment most travelers to Latin America indulge in is sightseeing, as every country has a vast offering of things to see that are of interest. The following phrases and vocabulary should help you get around:

Where is the tourism office located?
    ¿Dónde queda la oficina de turismo?
    (¿DOHN-day KAY-dah lah oh-fee-SEE-nah day too-REES-moh?)
Are there excursions to...?
    ¿Hay excursiones a...?
    (¿AH-ee eks-coor-see-OH-nays ah...?)
How can I hire a guide?
    ¿Cómo puedo contratar a un guía?
    (¿COH-moh PWAY-doh cohn-trah-TAHR ah oon GHEE-ah?)
What time does it open?
    ¿A qué hora se abre?
    (¿Ah kay OH-rah say AH-bray?)
What time does it close?
    ¿A qué hora se cierre?
    (¿Ah kay OH-rah say see-AY-ray?)

Places of interest:

archaeological ruins
    ruinas arqueológicas
    (roo-EE-nahs ahr-kay-oh-LOH-hee-cahs)
museum
    museo

(moo-SAY-oh)

market
> mercado
> (mayr-CAH-doh)

church
> iglesia
> (ee-GLAY-see-ah)

cathedral
> catedral
> (cah-tay-DRAHL)

palace
> palacio
> (pah-LAH-see-oh)

pyramids
> pirámides
> (pee-RAH-mee-days)

Theater

Even if your Spanish is not up to seeing a play, you most likely would enjoy a night at theater when the program is musical. In buying tickets, you'll need some of the following vocabulary:

ticket
> boleto
> (boh-LAY-toh)

row
> fila
> (FEE-lah)

right
> derecha
> (day-RAY-chah)

center
> centro
> (SAYN-troh)

left

izquierda

(ees-key-AYR-dah)

orchestra seat

luneta

(loo-NAY-tah)

box

palco

(PAHL-coh)

gallery

galería

(gah-lay-REE-ah)

The usher, or *acomodador*, who seats you should be given a small tip.

Night Clubs

The large luxury clubs in the major cities of Latin America often feature outstanding international stars. If you're interested in catching one of these performances, inquire at your hotel by asking:

Do you know of a club where we can see a good show?

¿Puede recomendar un club que tenga un buen show/espectáculo?

(¿PWAY-day ray-coh-mayn-DAHR oon cloob kay TAYN-gah oon bwayn shoh/ess-payk-TAH-coo-loh?)

Other questions you'll want to ask:

Is there a cover charge?

¿Hay una cuota de entrada?

(¿AH-ee OO-nah KWOH-tah day ayn-TRAH-dah?)

Mex. ¿un cóver?
(¿oon COH-vayr?)
Is there a minimum?

¿Hay un consumo mínimo?
(¿AH-ee oon cohn-SOO-moh MEE-nee-moh?)
When does the show begin?

¿Cuándo comienza el espectáculo?
(¿KWAN-doh coh-mee-AYN-sah el ess-payk-
TAH-coo-loh?)

What has become more difficult in recent times is to find performances of native folk music and dance. Travelers often report being frustrated when they attempt to find programs of this nature. Repeating the following phrase as often as possible may lead you to a place that features this type of entertainment:

Where is there a place where you can hear folk music?

¿Dónde hay un lugar en que se puede oír música folklórica?
(¿DOHN-day AH-ee oon loo-GAHR ayn kay say PWAY-day oh-EER MOO-see-cah folk-LOHR-ee-cah?)

Movies

Hollywood movies are widely distributed throughout Latin America, but expect to contend with the subtitles in Spanish. Another small, but annoying problem is that the audience often chats quite volubly during the film, because mostly they are reading rather than listening.

It's interesting to note that popular accompaniment to moviegoing, popcorn, is called something different in nearly every Latin American country. The following is a sampling:

Argentina - *pochoclo*
Bolivia - *pipocas*
Chile - *cabritas*
Colombia - *cristetas*
Cuba - *rositas de maíz*
Ecuador - *canguil*
Mexico - *palomitas*
Panama - *popcorn*
Peru *popcorn*
Venezuela - *cotufas*

The above was just for fun. All you'll have to do is point to get what you want.

SPORTS

Sports, both of the participatory and spectator types, are popular throughout Latin America. If you are a sports enthusiast, you'll want to know some of the following vocabulary:

Water Sports

swimming
natación
(nah-tah-see-OHN)
swimming pool
piscina
(pee-CEE-nah)

Mex. alberca
(ahl-BAYR-cah)

snorkel
snorkel
(snork-AYL)
scuba diving
bucear
(boo-say-AHR)
sailboat
velero
(vay-LAY-roh)
boat
lancha
(LAHN-chah)

Tennis

rachet
raqueta
(rah-KAY-tah)

ball
    pelota
    (pay-LOH-tah)
court
    cancha
    (CAHN-chah)
net
    red
    (rayd)

Golf

clubs
    palos
    (PAH-lohs)
ball
    bola
    (BOH-lah)
irons
    fierros
    (fee-AY-rohs)
woods
    maderas
    (mah-DAY-rahs)

Fishing

line
    línea
    (LEE-nay-ah)
hook
    gancho
    (GAHN-choh)
    or
    anzuelo
    (ahn-soo-AY-loh)

bait
    carnada
    (cahr-NAH-dah)
rod
    caña de pescar
    (CAH-nyah day pays-CAHR)

reel
    carrete
    (cahr-RAY-tay)
lure
    mosca
    (MOHS-cah)
net
    red
    (rayd)

Hunting

If you intend to bring hunting equipment into a Latin American country, be absolutely sure you have checked on their laws. More than one innocent hunter has gotten to know the inside of a foreign prison for not knowing the gun laws of the country they're visiting. If you are planning to hunt, it is much safer to rent your equipment there.

Here is a list of some game you may wish to hunt:

deer
    venado
    (vay-NAH-doh)
duck
    pato
    (PAH-toh)

goose
> ganso
> (GAHN-soh)

pheasant
> faisán
> (fah-ee-SAHN)

quail
> codorniz
> (coh-dohr-NEES)

dove
> paloma
> (pah-LOH-mah)

If you need to rent sports equipment, the following phrases will be useful:

Where can I rent gear for...
> ¿Dónde puedo alquilar equipo...
> (¿DOHN-day PWAY-doh ahl-key-LAHR ay-KEY-poh...)

> *Mex.* ¿ Dónde puedo rentar equipo...
> (¿DOHN-day PWAY-doh rayn-TAHR ay-KEY-poh...)

for hunting
> ...de caza?
> (...day CAH-sah?)

for fishing
> ...de pesca?
> (...day PAYS-cah?)

for water sports
> ...para deportes acúaticos?
> (...PAH-rah day-POHR-tays ah-KWAH-tee-cohs?)

for golf
> para golf?
> (PAH-rah golf?)

for tennis
> para tenis?
> (PAH-rah TAY-nees?)

Soccer

Many Latin Americans are fanatic followers of soccer, which they call *fútbol*. It's the most popular spectator sport played in the Spanish-speaking world.

Though American-style football is not played in Latin America, many people there follow it avidly on television and have their favorite U.S. teams. They call this game *fútbol americano* (FOOT-bohl ah-mayr-ee-CAH-noh) to differentiate it from soccer.

Jai Alai

Jai alai is a game which found its way to Latin America from the Basque country of Spain. Played on a three-sided court known as a *frontón* (frohn-TOHN), it's a game in which players throw and catch a small, hard, ball, or *pelota* (pay-LOH-tah), using a basket-like affair, or *cesta* (SAYS-tah), strapped to their arms. It's a very fast-paced game and quite dangerous. Furious betting takes place. If you've never seen the game, it's worth seeing at least once.

There will be no mention here of either the bullfight or the cockfight as there is nothing whatsoever "sporting" about them. The outcome is predetermined much to the detriment of the bulls and the cocks.

A FINAL BIT OF ADVICE

Don't be afraid to use the phrases in this book. The worst that can happen is that you won't be understood. The best that can happen is that you will.

In either case, your Latin American hosts will appreciate the fact that you tried.

Other Spanish Interest Titles from Hippocrene

SPANISH GRAMMAR
224 pages • 5½ x 8½ • ISBN 0-87052-893-9
• W • $12.95pb • (292)

SPANISH-ENGLISH/ ENGLISH-SPANISH PRACTICAL DICTIONARY
338 pages • 5½ x 8¼ • 35,000 entries
• ISBN 0-7818-0179-6 • NA • $9.95pb • (211)

SPANISH-ENGLISH/ ENGLISH-SPANISH CONCISE DICTIONARY (Latin America)
310 pages • 4 x 6 • 8,000 entries
• ISBN 0-7818-0261-x • W • $11.95pb • (258)

SPANISH-ENGLISH/ ENGLISH-SPANISH COMPACT DICTIONARY (Latin America)
310 pages • 3½ x 4¾ • 8,000 entries
• ISBN 0-7818-0497-3 • W • $8.95pb • (549)

MASTERING SPANISH
338 pages • 5½ X 8½ • ISBN 0-87052-059-8
• USA • $11.95 • (527)
2 cassettes: ISBN 0-87052-067-9 • USA
• $12.95 • (426)

MASTERING ADVANCED SPANISH
326 pages • 5½ x 8½ • ISBN 0-7818-0081-1
• W $14.95pb • (413)
2 cassettes: ISBN 0-7818-0089-7 • W
• $12.95 • (426)

SPANISH HANDY DICTIONARY
120 pages 5 x 7¾ • ISBN 0-7818-0012-9 • W
• $8.95pb • (189)

SPANISH-ENGLISH/ ENGLISH-SPANISH DICTIONARY OF COMPUTER TERMS
120 pages • 5½ x 8½ • 5,700 entries
• ISBN 0-7818-0148-6 • W • $16.95hc • (36)

SPANISH PROVERBS, IDIOMS AND SLANG

350 pages • 6 x 9 • ISBN 0-7818-0675-5 • W
• $14.95pb • (760)

DICTIONARY OF 1,000 SPANISH PROVERBS

131 pages • 5½ x 8½ • bilingual
• ISBN 0-7818-0412-4 • W • $11.95pb • (254)

TREASURY OF SPANISH LOVE

127 pages • 5 x 7 • ISBN 0-7818-0358-6 • W
• $11.95hc • (589)

2 cassettes • ISBN 0-7818-0365-9 • W
• $12.95hc • (584)

TREASURY OF CLASSIC SPANISH LOVE SHORT STORIES IN SPANISH AND ENGLISH

136 pages • 5x 7 • ISBN 0-7818-0512-0 • W
• $11.95hc • (604)

LANGUAGE AND TRAVEL GUIDE TO MEXICO

224 pages • 5 ½ x 8½ • ISBN 0-87052-622-7
• W • $14.95hc • (503)

HIPPOCRENE'S BEGINNER'S SERIES

Do you know what it takes to make a phone call in Russia? Or how to get through customs in Japan? This new language instruction series shows how to handle oneself in typical situations by introducing the business person or traveler not only to the vocabulary, grammar, and phrases of a new language, but also the history, customs, and daily practices of a foreign country.

The Beginner's Series consists of basic language instruction, which also includes vocabulary, grammar, and common phrases and review questions, along with cultural insights, interesting historical background, the country's basic facts and hints about everyday living-driving, shopping, eating out, and more.

BEGINNER'S ASSYRIAN
185 pages • 5 x 9 • 0-7818-0677-1
• $11.95pb • (763)

BEGINNER'S CHINESE
150 pages • 5½ x 8 • 0-7818-0566-x
• $14.95pb • (690)

BEGINNER'S BULGARIAN
207 pages • 5½ x 8½ • 0-7818-0300-4
• $9.95pb • (76)

BEGINNER'S CZECH
200 pages • 5½ x 8½ • 0-7818-0231-8
• $9.95pb • (74)

BEGINNER'S ESPERANTO
400 pages • 5½ x 8½ • 0-7818-0230-x
• $14.95pb • (51)

BEGINNER'S HUNGARIAN
200 pages • 5½ x 7 • 0-7818-0209-1
• $7.95pb • (68)

BEGINNER'S JAPANESE
200 pages • 5½ x 8½ • 0-7818-0234-2
• $11.95pb • (53)

BEGINNER'S LITHUANIAN
230 pages • 6 x 9 • 0-7818-0678-X
• $19.95pb • (764)

BEGINNER'S MAORI
121 pages • 5½ x 8½ • 0-7818-0605-4
• $8.95pb • (703)

BEGINNER'S PERSIAN
150 pages • 5½ x 8 • 0-7818-0567-8
• $14.95pb • (696)

BEGINNER'S POLISH
200 pages • 5½ x 8½ • 0-7818-0299-7
• $9.95pb • (82)
BEGINNER'S ROMANIAN
200 pages • 5½ x 8½ • 0-7818-0208-3
• $7.95pb • (79)
BEGINNER'S RUSSIAN
200 pages • 5½ x 8½ • 0-7818-0232-6
• $9.95pb • (61)
BEGINNER'S SICILIAN
158 pages • 5½ x 8½ • 0-7818-0640-2
• $11.95pb • (7 16)
BEGINNER'S SWAHILI
200 pages • 5½ x 8½ • 0-7818-0335-7
• $9.95pb • (52)
BEGINNER'S UKRAINIAN
130 pages • 5½ x 8½ • 0-7818-0443-4
• $11.95pb • (88)
BEGINNER'S VIETNAMESE
517 pages • 7 x 10 • 30 lessons • 0-7818-0411-6
• $19.95pb • (253)
BEGINNER'S WELSH
210 pages • 5½ x 8½ • 0-7818-0589-9
• $9.95pb • (712)

THE DICTIONARY & PHRASEBOOK SERIES
AUSTRALIAN DICTIONARY AND PHRASEBOOK
131 pages • 3¾ x 7 • 1,500 entries
• 0-7818-0539-2 • W • $11.95pb • (626)
BASQUE-ENGLISH/ ENGLISH-BASQUE DICTIONARY AND PHRASEBOOK
240 pages • 3¾ x 7 • 1,500 entries
• 0-7818-0622-4 • W • $11.95pb • (751)

**BOSNIAN-ENGLISH/ENGLISH-BOSNIAN
DICTIONARY AND PHRASEBOOK**
175 pages • 3¾ x 7 • 1,500 entries
• 0-7818-0596-1 • W • $11.95pb • (691)
**BRETON-ENGLISH/ENGLISH-BRETON
DICTIONARY AND PHRASEBOOK**
131 pages • 3¾ x 7 • 1,500 entries
• 0-7818-0540-6 • W • $11.95pb • (627)
**BRITISH-AMERICAN/
AMERICAN-BRITISH
DICTIONARY AND PHRASEBOOK**
160 pages • 3¾2 x 7 • 1,400 entries
• 0-7818-0450-7 • W • $11.95pb • (247)
**CHECHEN-ENGLISH/
ENGLISH-CHECHEN
DICTIONARY AND PHRASEBOOK**
160 pages • 3¾x 7 • 1,400 entries
• 0-7818-0446-9 • NA • $11.95pb • (183)
**GEORGIAN-ENGLISH/
ENGLISH-GEORGIAN
DICTIONARY AND PHRASEBOOK**
150 pages • 3¾ x 7 • 1,300 entries
• 0-7818-0542-2 • W • $11.95pb • (630)
**EASTERN ARABIC-ENGLISH/
ENGLISH-EASTERN ARABIC
DICTIONARY AND PHRASEBOOK**
142 pages • 3¾ x 7 • 2,200 entries
• 0-7818-0685-2 • W • $11.95pb • (774)
**ILOCANO-ENGLISH/ENGLISH-ILOCANO
DICTIONARY AND PHRASEBOOK**
174pages • 5 x 8 • 0-7818-0642-9
• $11.95pb • (718)
**IRISH-ENGLISH/ENGLISH-IRISH
DICTIONARY AND PHRASEBOOK**
160 pages • 3¾2 x 7 • 1,400 entries/phrases
• 0-87052-110-1 NA • $7.95pb • (385)

**LINGALA-ENGLISH/ENGLISH-LINGALA
DICTIONARY AND PHRASEBOOK**
120 pages • 3¾ x 7 • 0-7818-0456-6 • W
• $11.95pb • (296)
**MALTESE-ENGLISH/ENGLISH-MALTESE
DICTIONARY AND PHRASEBOOK**
175 pages • 3¾ x 7 • 1,500 entries
• 0-7818-0565-1 • W • $11.95pb • (697)
**POLISH DICTIONARY AND
PHRASEBOOK**
252 page • 5½ x 8½ • 0-7818-0134-6 • W
• $11.95pb • (192)
**RUSSIAN DICTIONARY AND
PHRASEBOOK, Revised**
256 pages • 5½ x 8½ • 3,000 entries
• 0-7818-0190-7 • W • $9.95pb • (597)
**SLOVAK-ENGLISH/ENGLISH-SLOVAK
DICTIONARY AND PHRASEBOOK**
180 pages • 3¾ x 7 • 1,300 entries
• 0-7818-0663-1 • W • $13.95pb • (754)
**UKRAINIAN DICTIONARY AND
PHRASEBOOK**
205 pages • 5½ x 8½ • 3,000 entries
• 0-7818-0188-5• $11.95pb • (28)

All prices are subject to change without prior
notice. To order Hippocrene Books, contact
your local bookstore, call (718) 454-2366, or
write to: Hippocrene Books, 171 Madison Ave.
New York, NY 10016. Please enclose check or
money order adding $5.00 shipping (UPS) for
the first book and $.50 for each additional
title.

$11.95

Spanish-English/ English-Spanish Dictionary and Phrasebook
(Latin America)
Ila Warner

This dictionary and phrasebook covers the Spanish dialects found throughout the Caribbean and Central and South America. The book includes a dictionary of over 2,000 words, followed by a brief introduction to (Latin American) Spanish grammar. The helpful phrasebook chapters cover all topics a traveler needs to know, including transportation, shopping, eating out, and much more. There are also comments on culture and lifestyle.

HIPPOCRENE BOOKS, INC.
171 Madison Avenue
New York, NY 10016